Animals in Play

Barry Nicholson

Starhands Publishing

CONTENTS

Contents
List of Play Scripts

page 22   Paul the Psychic Octopus
page 29   Dick Whittington and His Cat
page 36   Famous Animals from Britain
page 45   The Musicians of Bremen
page 52   The Legend of the Golden Duck
page 59   The Dragon of Krakow
page 65   Greek Mythological Animals
page 73   Lucky Animals of Italy
page 81   The Wooden Horse of Troy
page 88   Noah's Ark
page 97   Endangered! The Indian Elephant
page 104   The Cat Who Came Late to the Party
page 111   Interesting Idioms
page 118   Clever Camouflage
page 126   Herbal Remedies for Animals
page 134   Can Birds Think?

References
About the Author
From the Same Author

LIST OF PLAY SCRIPTS

PAUL THE PSYCHIC OCTOPUS – *page 24*

DICK WHITTINGTON AND HIS CAT – *page 31*

MEET THE FAMOUS ANIMALS FROM BRITAIN – *page 40*

THE MUSICIANS OF BREMEN – *page 47*

THE LEGEND OF THE GOLDEN DUCK – *page 54*

THE DRAGON OF KRAKOW – *page 61*

HOW TO KILL A MYTHICAL BEAST – *page 68*

THE ROOSTERS WHO SAVED THE PARTY – *page 77*

THE TROJAN HORSE – *page 84*

NOAH'S ARK – *page 92*

THE THREE ELEPHANTS – *page 100*

THE CAT WHO CAME LATE TO THE PARTY – *page 106*

NAME THAT ANIMAL IDIOM – *page 114*

THE CAMOUFLAGE HOMEWORK PROJECT – *page 121*

GOOD FOR YOU, BAD FOR YOU? – *page 130*

CAN BIRDS THINK? – *page 137*

Introduction

Welcome!

Who doesn't love animals? They are playful, innocent, and reflect many human character traits. In this book you will find sixteen stories from the animal world, each accompanied by a play script designed for young learners. Children and teens will enjoy acting out the skits, and will wake up to the joys of animal stories through practical drama and literature.

Play, Story and Skit

A few words in the book's title need defining: play, story and skit. The definitions have been drawn from various online dictionaries (see the reference list at the back of the book for details).

Play: In a theatrical sense, it is a piece of writing intended to be acted in a theatre or similar place of performance; it is a dramatic work for stage or to be broadcast. An intriguing alternative definition sees 'play' as a light or brisk, constantly changing movement, as in 'a play of light'; or on an even higher level as freedom of action or activity, as in 'a full play of the mind'. Whereas I do not expect our students to encounter this higher state of being, it would, however, be nice if their creative juices were squeezed and stretched a little.

Story: We often ask our students to write a story or order a sequence of events so that they make sense, and we usually use the past simple to achieve this. Essentially, a 'story' is a narrative, either true of fictional, designed to interest, amuse, or instruct the reader; and this is often a connected series of events that can be either true or imagined.

Skit: A 'skit' is a satirical or humorous story or sketch, especially one done by amateurs. It derives from the word 'sketch', and is often a comedic segment of a show or performance that often makes a joke of something. Certainly this element of humour is a theme that crops up throughout this book, and your children or teens will no doubt be eager to tap in to this valuable way of viewing the world at large.

A lot of the definitions suggest some kind of public performance, for example on TV or radio. Though I realise this is beyond the capability of most of us in the classroom or community centre, it may be possible to experiment with a video camera or other audio-visual recording device as resources and technology allow. Failing that, a well-rehearsed public performance will certainly do!

Scope and style

This book is primarily aimed at parents, teachers, and youth community leaders and their child or children, but there is also much of interest to the general reader. The stories and skits are written in a simple and enjoyable way, but do not patronise the reader or student.

Thankfully English is an art, not a science; it is descriptive rather than prescriptive; it is a creative and cultural act. Throughout, the English language is taken as a creative being; an abstract entity that can be neither seen nor heard except in its manifestation as the written word or spoken utterance. This is expressed no more so than in a short play or skit. And, as Shakespeare would have it, "all the world's a stage, and all the men and women mere players" ('As You Like It' Act II Scene VII). I want to motivate and inspire – that means teachers, parents and youth leaders as well as children and teens – and it is in this light that this book has been written. Though it does not claim to be *the* answer, or even *an* answer, the book does claim to be a *way*, a way to approach your lessons or study period through literature, stories and drama.

The real question is one of motivation, of getting students motivated to study, and to help them help their peers to success too. The skills our youngsters get in these early days will help propel them into the future – their future – towards high school, university and beyond. As they progress through time, the study skills, methods and motivation techniques we show them now will stick with them and be added to and developed by them; education, drama and story-telling skills that will stay with and guide them, that they themselves can pass on to others.

Students can then progress in their studies with a sense of purpose and confidence.

Structure and Layout

Each unit follows the same basic pattern. After the title there is a short summary of the story called 'In Brief'. Here, the story is told, mostly in past simple and in prose. It is designed to be read either in one's head or out loud, perhaps before an audience or class of students in assembly.

Then the play script itself. First there is a list of characters that appear in the play – some are human, some animals, and some things. Then the setting is given, which gives ideas for scenery; then the script. I have tried to keep stage directions to a minimum or, in some circumstances not at all, when directions are obvious and so obsolete. The 'Director's Corner' gives further suggestions for the set, costumes, props, lighting and sound (see the section below).

As a parent, teacher or youth leader, it is your creative juices that are equally as important as the children's, and so you should feel free to adapt or add to the presented materials if you judge it to be correct, according to your opinion, resources, and working environment.

The Stories

The stories are divided into four main themes, three geographical regions and one academic section:

> ❖ *Western Europe*
> ❖ *Eastern Europe and the Mediterranean*
> ❖ *Asia*
> ❖ *Academic and Intellectual*

Each theme presents four stories (and following them, four plays or skits). In more detail the sixteen units are:

1. Paul the Psychic Octopus
   Paul was a 'psychic' octopus who successfully predicted the results of World Cup football matches, becoming a social media phenomenon;

2. Dick Whittington and His Cat

Dick Whittington famously overcame poverty to become the Lord Mayor of London, alongside his trusty cat;

3. Famous Animals from Britain

Famous animals come from all around the world, and here I focus on some of the best from Britain;

4. The Musicians of Bremen

A donkey, dog, cat and rooster decide to make their way to Bremen to become musicians;

5. The Legend of the Golden Duck

A talking duck gives money to Jacob on condition that he only spends it on himself. However, he gives a gold coin to a beggar upon which all his wealth disappears;

6. The Dragon of Krakow

Some youngsters disturbed a dragon and it became very angry. A villager, Krakus, managed to slay the dragon, and has the city named after him;

7. Greek Mythological Animals

No country has more mythological animals than (ancient) Greece, some of them good, some of them bad, and some of them ugly;

8. Lucky Animals of Italy

The Italian wolf is lucky in Rome, the rooster is lucky in Florence, and the elephant is lucky in Sicily;

9. The Wooden Horse of Troy

The story signifies trickery in order to win a battle, and echoes the saying 'beware of Greeks bearing gifts';

10. Noah's Ark

Noah built an ark to escape the floods and filled it with animals. It finally settled on Mount Arafat in eastern Turkey;

11. Endangered! Elephants of India

Though they are revered, there has been a steady decline in elephant numbers and increasing concerns about their welfare;

12. The Cat Who Came Late to the Party

There is no Chinese year of the cat, and the reason is explained In this mythical story;

13. Interesting Idioms

Sometimes we can't express what we think or feel, but idioms allow this through imagery or a short anecdote;

14. Clever Camouflage

Camouflage, the art of not being seen, is widely employed in the animal world, especially to evade predators or sneak up on prey;

15. Herbal Remedies for Animals

Some remedies work well for humans, but how far can they be used for animals?

16. Can Birds Think?

There's a lot of debate about whether birds can think, show emotions, or even possess a sense of humour.

The Props / Costume Box

Children and teens have great imagination and, at this level, simple props and costumes will do. Let us look at the two concepts – props and costumes – in turn, and note how, for our purposes, the 'props box' and 'costume box' are one and the same.

Props are an essential part of any staged performance, and can be elaborate and complicated or as simple as a table and chair. Usually a skit or short play designed for (or written by) children or teens will veer towards the latter, making use of whatever is in the classroom or community centre. That is not to say that a few well-chosen and placed props would not enhance the performance. Think plastic daggers and tomato ketchup for a murder-mystery, for example.

Sharman (2004) identifies a 'props table' and defines a 'prop' as "practically everything on the set that is not nailed down – from the pictures on the walls to the contents of a handbag". Sharman divides props into the following categories:

1. Furniture – tables, chairs, sofas, beds, etc.;
2. Glass (and Pottery) – bottles, glasses, flower pots, etc.;
3. Food & Drink – both real and fake;
4. Flowers & Plants – as part of the set, or as part of the play;
5. Personal Props – eg. the contents of a handbag, or cigarettes.

To which I add:

1. Classroom-related Props – desks, chairs, blackboard, etc.;

2. Breakable or Broken Props – that may be broken as part of the script (eg. a jug thrown to the floor);
3. Intellectual Props – things spoken about but not seen;
4. People as Props – eg. children dressed as trees in the background;
5. Wearable Props – eg. a pair of glasses, or a wig.

Let's move on to the 'costume' part of the box. As I mentioned before (and as you will no doubt already know), children and teens have a marvellous capacity for creativity and imagination. At this level simple costumes, often just one or two fancy dressing-up clothes, if anything, will do. The question of make-up will probably not arise at all.

So, keep it simple – the simpler the better – and remember that you only have to *suggest* a character by their appearance: you're not going for a Hollywood Oscar. Take the example of 'The Musicians of Bremen'. You only need to suggest to the audience that the four students standing in front of you are the four animals in the story, or that the two teenagers are cut-throat robbers – the audience's imagination will do the rest! The donkey, dog, cat and rooster might have a simple costume such as a mask, or the robbers a stripy T-shirt and face mask, for instance.

For our purposes the prop box and costume box are combined. I'd recommend you get an old (large) cardboard box from the local supermarket, or arrange all the bits and bobs on a table (as Sharman suggests). I prefer a large cardboard box because it is portable and introduces an element of 'lucky dip'.

If you really want to make a professional go of it, you can assign a 'props table', labelled as such, marking it out with masking tape according to scene. In our example 'The Musicians of Bremen', most of the props and costumes are the same throughout the scenes, so it is not necessary to lay them out scene-by-scene, but instead 'all in one go'. You could go so far as to label each area of the table according to what prop or costume piece should be placed there. Laying out the table can be assigned as the job for the 'props team'.

Lighting and Sound Effects

Lighting, in a short children or teen's play performed in front of peers, may not be a consideration at all. But a few of the skits presented in this book could do with a sprinkle of lighting effects so to enhance dramatic effect. I am primarily thinking of a few examples.

For 'How to Kill a Mythical Beast' the backdrop of the Acropolis can be lit brightly and the yellow or light green hills can be lit more gently. A different coloured light can be used to light up each of the three beasts (Hydra, Medusa and Minotaur). In the up-beat play 'Good For You, Bad For You?' the quiz show atmosphere can be created with a sparkly, starry set that can be lit up with a variety of colours to great effect. Finally, take the example of 'The Dragon of Krakow' with its dark, spooky, rocky cave. Lighting will be minimal, perhaps the flicker of a candle or small torch. But there is a sudden fire-like flash when the dragon appears!

I am not anticipating that your students will use sound effects other than the very simplest. You might, for example, use a hand-bell to signify the ring of the church bells in 'Dick Whittington and His Cat', or the taped trumpet of an elephant in 'The Three Elephants'. Some of the plays involve several scenes, and the gaps between them (when costumes and furniture are being changed) could be filled with interlude music such as between the scenes in 'The Legend of the

Golden Duck'. But sound effects and music for our purposes are a luxury, not a necessity.

The Director's Corner

The 'Director' could either be you, or one of the students themselves. If they are to work in small groups and write and produce their own play or skit then the role of the director is far less important. On the other hand, if there is to be a final performance in front of parents and/or peers, then the choice of a confident director who can, literally, direct, becomes paramount. I think that within the scope of this book, it can be assumed that the 'adult' will be named the director.

OK, so what kind of things does a director do? Essentially, they plan the whole thing from start to finish, from choice of who plays what part, to saying who stands or moves where on stage. This is not to say that the children or teens will have no say in anything – on the contrary, it is partially the director's role to listen to and incorporate ideas and suggestions if they are appropriate. But at the end of the day, the director has the final say.

Take a look at some of the sub-sections of the introduction: the props and costume box, lighting and sound effects, set design, and also matters such as getting everyone in the right place at the right time, someone falling ill and not being able to take part, or a change of classroom or venue at the last moment. These are all the responsibility of the director. So, the director must have a firm overview of proceedings and a clear idea of 'the big picture'.

It depends on your circumstances, of course, but sometimes the students can be set up in small groups of, say, four or five, and told to get on with it by themselves. It is a good idea in this case to give the students some guidance as to how to go about the task, maybe a printed handout with a sequence of things to do: name of the play, character list, who is to be set and scenery manager, costume designer, script writer, and so on. It is a good idea for the group to elect a 'group leader' from the outset – a kind of pseudo-director.

Whoever is directing, or leading, someone will have to come up with some sort of a basic set. I'm not suggesting lavish backdrops lit with super-troopers and glitterballs (can you imagine?) – a table and chair will do. You might like to put up some cardboard hills behind Dick Whittington, or some trees behind The Musicians of Bremen, for example. Keep it simple, and remember that what the audience can see is less defined compared to what you can all see on stage!

Moving Forward

Everyone loves animals, no-one more so than children. There are lots of opportunities to get out and about and mix with animals: zoos, nature trails, cat cafes, petting farms, to name but a few. Most of the stories in this book can be tied to a geographical location, and it makes sense to plan your excursion according to topic. For example a project on 'Paul the Psychic Octopus' and animal intelligence can be accompanied by a visit to the local aquarium; or why not visit Chinatown to supplement 'The Cat Who Came Late To The Party'? These visits will have the effect that the stories and plays come to life!

What more can I say? Enjoy this collection of diamonds from the animal kingdom, and all things considered your students will enjoy them too.

Barry Nicholson
London 2020

Paul the Psychic Octopus

In Brief

Paul was a 'psychic' octopus who could successfully predict the result of World Cup football matches. He correctly predicted all of Germany's matches in the 2010 competition, becoming a star and major social media phenomenon.

The playful, eight-legged mollusc was born at the Sea Life Centre, Weymouth (UK), on 26th January 2008, but soon moved to his permanent home at the Sea Life Aquarium in Oberhausen, Germany. It was here that his amazing talent was revealed.

As a coffee break prank his keepers lowered two boxes into his tank, one with Germany's flag and one with Poland's flag: the two football teams that were playing that day. Each box contained a tasty snack, and the keepers joked that whichever box Paul picked first would win the match. To their amazement, Paul plumped for Germany – who duly won! Was this just a lucky 'guess' or was there something more profound at play?

We don't know how he did it, but Paul the octopus correctly predicted the outcome of all six of Germany's matches, *plus* Germany's 3rd place play-off, *and* the winner of the World Cup itself. Of these, Paul famously predicted Germany's first-round defeat at the hands of Serbia, and the team's semi-final defeat against the eventual winners, Spain!

Paul became a celebrity on TV and social media. His tank was surrounded by scores of fans and journalists, and home TV channel NTV started airing his predictions live. His trends on Twitter were high. The 'eight-armed-oracle' was an even bigger hit in Spain, being offered a 'holiday' at Madrid Zoo, and an honorary citizenship of a Spanish town.

So, how did Paul *know* which of the two boxes to choose? Some suggested that tastier snacks were put into the winning (often German) box. Others suggested that Paul simply preferred stripy flags. Others put it all down to basic probability theory. Germany's leading octopus researcher wondered if Paul was affected by different-sized mussels or flavours. But most people believed in his genuine predictive powers.

Paul made better World cup predictions than Goldman Sachs, with a success rate of 100% compared to the latter's meagre 35.5%, proving instinct to be better than technological analytics. Not bad for a sea creature who had never set a tentacle on the pitch, eh?

Take a look on the internet for some interesting snippets, including a site that invites the user to ask Paul a difficult life question, with such thrilling choices as 'Should I ask him/her out?', 'Will I go bald?', and 'Should I get a dog?' (yes, no, no, in my case). I found two 'Paul the Octopus' songs, one official by Parry Gipp ("your tentacles are magical"); the other a Spanish official version in which brightly-clothed young men and attendant puppets play musical instruments and dance around some bloke in an octopus costume. You have been warned!

Back in the real world at the aquarium in Oberhausen, there is a permanent shrine: an enormous fibre-glass Paul balanced on an oversized and very colourful football, his playful tentacles dangling all over. More down to earth for us is a visit to our local aquarium or zoo.

Play: Paul the Psychic Octopus

Characters

Paul the Octopus
zookeeper
journalists
boy
girl

Setting

Paul's tank, decorated with footballs, coral and seaweed.

Script

Zookeeper: Good morning, Paul.
Paul: Good morning, zookeeper.
Zookeeper: Are you feeling clever today?
Paul: Oh, I get it. Another football match, right?
Zookeeper: That's right. But don't tell the people that you can speak English.
Paul: OK. Who's playing?
Zookeeper: Germany and Poland.
Paul: *(he thinks)* Hmmmm, interesting…

***

Boy: Look! Here's Paul's tank!
Girl: Yes. There he is!
Boy: Wow! He is a golden colour!

Girl: With eight golden tentacles!
Boy: What's he doing?
Girl: I don't know. Let's watch…
(the boy and girl watch intently)

***

Journalist: OK, here are two boxes, Paul. Will you choose Germany or Poland?
(Paul waves his tentacles, then chooses the 'Poland' box)
Paul: This one!
Journalist: He chose Poland! He chose Poland!
Keeper: Well done, Paul.
Boy: I don't believe it! Germany are much better than Poland!
Girl: Yes. Germany will win. Paul is wrong!
(they watch the big screen TV)
Commentator: Goal! Poland are the winners!
Boy & Girl: I don't believe it!

***

Journalist: OK, here are two boxes, Paul. Will you choose Germany or Serbia?
(Paul waves his tentacles, then chooses the Serbia box)
Paul: This one!
Journalist: He chose Serbia! He chose Serbia!
Keeper: Well done, Paul.
Boy: I don't believe it! Germany are much better than Serbia!
Girl: Yes. Germany will win. Paul is wrong!
(they watch the big screen TV)
Commentator: Goal! Serbia are the winners!
Boy & Girl: I don't believe it!

***

Journalist: OK, here are two more boxes, Paul. Will you choose
Germany or Spain?
(Paul waves his tentacles, then chooses the Spain box)
Paul: This one!
Journalist: He chose Spain! He chose Spain!
Keeper: Well done, Paul.
Boy: I don't believe it! Germany are much better than Spain!
Girl: Yes. Germany will win. Paul is wrong!
(they watch the big screen TV)
Commentator: Goal! Spain are the winners!
Boy & Girl: I don't believe it!

***

Keeper: Well done, Paul. You made a lot of money.
Paul: Really? That's good. But please don't tell anyone that I speak
English!
(all actors gather on stage and sing Paul's song...)
Everyone: *Paul the octopus, Paul the octopus, Paul the octopus, we love
you...*

(All actors take a bow)

Director's Corner

The main character is Paul, and how fancy you make his costume is up to you – so long as he is able to move around and wave his arms. You can put Paul in a tank or better still make the whole set into an underwater scene. The two boxes that Paul chooses from can be in clear view at the front, and decorated in the teams' colours or national flag (Germany, Poland, Serbia and Spain). Try increasing the tension as Paul chooses his box by pausing, thinking, or playing music to suggest indecision.

The Set
 ✓ *seaweed, rocks and small fish in the background*
 ✓ *a tank (or the whole set can be the tank?)*

Costumes and Props Box
 ✓ *an octopus costume – use long socks or stockings stuffed with newspaper for the arms*
 ✓ *boxes decorated with the teams' national flags*
 ✓ *zookeeper's costume (long coat, hat and net)*
 ✓ *a camera for the journalist (a card box?)*
 ✓ *a big screen TV (a box)*

Sound and Lighting
 ✓ *recording of crowd cheering as the goals are scored*

Other Considerations
 ✓ *search for a 'Paul the Octopus' song on the internet*
 ✓ *Can you find any other 'psychic' animals – there are lots of them!*

Dick Whittington and His Cat

In Brief

One of the most well-known characters of British folklore is Dick Whittington. He famously overcame poverty and a third-class lifestyle to become the Lord Mayor of London. But it was not his intention – it was only when he tried to leave London that the church bells called him back with the iconic words "Turn again, Whittington, Lord Mayor of London". Incredibly, he kept his obedient cat, Boots, with him throughout the saga, and it was the cat's ability to catch mice and rats that helped a young Dick to his prestigious post.

Dick Whittington was born in the countryside and for the first years of his life was poor, hungry and knew nothing of the city. He came to hear tales of London where the streets were paved with gold. With gold? His curiosity got the better of him and he set off with his trusty cat, Boots, to find his fortune.

But London was not what he expected: overcrowded, dirty streets, with a lot of people who had no time for him. What's more, the streets were not paved with gold! He eventually found work in a shop, moving boxes and delivering parcels to rich people. The job did not pay well, and his cat was little help in his toils. So Dick decided to leave and go back to his village. He said farewell to the shopkeeper and made his way north, into the rolling hills above London. But then something strange happened: as Dick and Boots walked up the steep slopes of Highgate Hill he heard the bells of Bow Church ring. They appeared to call to him, speaking the words "Turn again Whittington, Lord Mayor of London". Dick and Boots looked at each other. Could church bells really speak?

Surely not. But Dick took this as a sign and returned to the city.

He was amazed to find the place filled with unfriendly rats that ate all the people's food and destroyed their houses. Boots, however, did not see the problem and happily ran around town catching all the rats. The King noticed this and asked whose cat it was. It was Dick's. The King was very pleased, and immediately gave Dick his own horse, lots of gold, and made him Lord Mayor of London. Dick was a very worthy Lord Mayor, building houses, a college and a library for the poor. The King, Dick, Boots and all the city people were very happy.

What evidence of Dick Whittington can we see today? Probably most familiar are the many pantomimes that take up his story, often with a lot of humour. These pantomimes have their roots in the nineteenth century when this style of performance became popular. In London the Whittington Stone stands at the foot of Highgate Hill (close to the modern Wittington Stone pub). Though the stone was erected in 1821, the cat atop it was only added in 1964. In the City of London is St. Michael Patenoster Royal Church where Dick is buried; a plaque and stained glass window commemorate him. On College Hill nearby, there is another, similar plaque. Unfortunately, the exact location of Dick's grave has been lost over the years.

The Whittington Hospital (with its own trusty cat) stands on Highgate Hill, and is reputed to be the spot where Dick 'turned again'. Outside London, Whittington Castle stands in the village of Whittington, Shropshire. It was fully renovated and a tearoom and visitor attraction added in 2007, and was opened that year by the Duke of Gloucester. So don't ever give up – "turn again" just like Dick and Boots, and with perseverance you can achieve what you like!

Play: Dick Wittington and His Cat

Characters

Dick Whittington
Boots (Dick's Cat)
Shop Owner
King
The Church Bells
Rats (unspoken part)

Setting

Medieval London, timber-framed houses and cobbled streets, with green hills in the far distance

Script

Dick: Come on, Boots, let's go and find our fortune in London.
Boots: Meow! London?
Dick: Yes, Boots – London. They say the streets are paved with gold.
Boots: Meow! Gold? Meow!

***

Dick: *(to shop owner)* We are tired. We are hungry. Do you have a place for us to stay?
Shop Owner: Tired? Hungry? A place to stay? You have to work for your food and bed. Work!
Dick: OK. What shall I do?

Shop Owner: Move these boxes! Sweep the floor! Deliver these heavy boxes to the other side of town! Do it! Now!

Dick: Yes, yes, yes… *(Dick moves the boxes, sweeps the floor, and delivers the heavy boxes to the other side of town)* Boots, will you help me?

Boots: Meow! I'm a cat. I can't help. Sorry!

Dick: How about rats? Can you catch some rats?

Boots: Meow! No, I'm sleepy. When are we going home?

Dick: Let's go now. London is hard work, and this shop owner pays very little money. *(they walk up into the green hills; they hear something…)*

Church Bells: Dick, Dick, listen. Don't go, don't go. Come back to London, you will be rich, come back to London, you will be famous, turn again Dick Wittington, Lord Mayor of London!

Dick: What? Did the church bells speak to me?

Boots: Meow! Yes, I think they did!

Dick: I will not give up! I will not leave London!

Church Bells: Turn again, Wittington, Lord Mayor of London!

***

Boots: Meow! Look, a fine house. A fine house with lots of rats. I can help. I can catch all the rats. *(Boots chases and catches all the rats)*

King: Look! All the rats are gone! Whose cat is this?

Dick: It is my cat, Your Majesty. My name is Dick.

King: Your cat is a very good cat. And you are a good boy, Dick. Please stay here with your cat and keep the rats away!

Boots: Meow! Yes, thank you, King.

King: And you, Dick, will be my Lord Mayor of London.

Dick: Yes, thank you, King. *(the King presents Dick and Boots with fine clothes and horses and lots of gold; they are all happy)*

King: *(speaks to audience)* Maybe next time it will be your turn?

Everybody: Hooray for the King! Hooray for Boots! Hooray for Dick Wittington, Lord Mayor of London! *(they all clap and cheer)*.

(All actors take a bow)

Director's Corner

You can use one set for all the parts, maybe hills on the left, medieval houses on the right. The part of Boots could be played by a (suitably dressed) student, or a toy cat can be used with the spoken words voiced over – it depends how many people are at hand. The King could be sitting on a throne, and he can also give a 'horse' for Boots to ride, which could be quite humorous!

The Set
- ✓ *hills and woods*
- ✓ *medieval (timber-framed) buildings*

Costumes and Props Box
- ✓ *boxes and a broom*
- ✓ *toy rat(s)*
- ✓ *hand-bell(s)*
- ✓ *some gold coins*
- ✓ *King's crown and red robe (think 'curtains')*
- ✓ *Lord Mayor's hat and robe*
- ✓ *horses (large cardboard cut-outs?)*

Sound and Lighting
- ✓ *church bells (represented by hand-bells?)*

Other considerations
- ✓ *do not use a real cat ;-)*
- ✓ *the moral is that, with perseverance, you can achieve anything you want*

Famous Animals from Britain

In Brief

Who doesn't like animals? Kids, teens and adults alike find fascination and comfort in our little (and big) friends, and it has been proven that human contact with animals reduces stress and anxiety, and lowers blood pressure and heart rate. Famous animals come from all round the world, but here I focus on some of the very best from Britain.

Many of the most famous have lived in London Zoo, located within Regent's Park in London. Top of the list are two very special animals, both very different. Guy the gorilla was born on Guy Fawkes Day 1947 (hence the name) and arrived at the zoo as a baby, clutching a mini hot water bottle. You can easily find this image on the internet as it is very famous. He became instantly popular with an adoring public, who travelled from afar to see him. When sparrows entered his enclosure, he would scoop them up gently, peer at them, then let them go. Cute! After he died in 1978, a statue was erected near his old enclosure that visitors can see to this day.

In 1965 another of London Zoo's animals shot to fame – Goldie, the golden eagle. Why? Because the plucky bird managed to escape and spent a total of eleven days, 19½ hours 'on the run' in Regent's Park before finally being coaxed back to the zoo by friendly zookeepers. Such was Goldie's fame that he was cheered every time he was mentioned in the House of Commons, and 5,000 spectators caused traffic jams and havoc around Regent's Park as they flocked to try and see him. More animals from London Zoo later.

Eros was a wild snowy owl who got lost at sea near the Azores, mid-Atlantic. He fell exhausted onto the deck of HMS Eros (hence the name) where the crew took him as their mascot. He lived for many years and fathered 57 chicks with three different mates before his sad death in 1993.

Belinda was a Mexican red-kneed bird-eating spider who, despite appearances, was very human-friendly and became very popular with the public. She made countless TV appearances, helping people overcome their fear of spiders, and as part of hypnotherapy programmes. She also died in 1993, aged 22 years.

Back to London Zoo, Winnie was an American black bear donated to the zoo at the outbreak of World War I in 1914. She was often visited by the author A.A. Milne and his son Christopher, and was the inspiration for Winnie the Pooh and Christopher Robin.

Staying on a bear theme, Brumas was a polar bear born on 27th November 1949, named after her keepers Bruce and Sam. She was apparently the first polar bear to be successfully raised in Britain, and caused much interest – London Zoo's attendance skyrocketed by one million in the year 1950, for example. She was the inspiration for many souvenirs, books, and toys – we have her to thank for the gift shops we always see at visitor attractions around the world. Pipaluk ("the little one") was another polar bear at the zoo, born on 1st December 1967. He attracted many spectators until he left in 1985 to retire to a zoo in Poland.

Jumbo the elephant was born in 1861 and, along with his companion Alice, were trained to give people of all ages rides on their backs. This was quite amazing as the elephants were each 11 feet tall. What a view! Jumbo and his companion were well-known for their playful nature, stealing people's hats before gently replacing them on their owner's heads. Sadly, he died in 1885, but his name lives on in the form of those giant flying machines, 'jumbo jets'.

Back at sea, Unsinkable Sam was a cat who was just that – unsinkable. During World War II he survived three great ship sinkings. First, the German ship Bismarck which sank on 27th May 1941; then he was saved by the HMS Cossack which itself sank on 24th October that same year; and Sam's last ship, HMS Ark Royal was again sunk off Gibraltar. Apparently she was rescued "angry but quite unharmed". Unsinkable indeed.

Well, that was an unsinkable cat. But how about an unsinkable pig? That's just who Tirpitz was. She was saved from the German ship SMS Dresden when it sank in 1915, by the HMS Glasgow. One of the crew risked his life to jump in to rescue her, and the over-sized pig became the ship's mascot. Though she died soon after the end of the war, she was stuffed and donated to the Imperial War Museum.

Gustav was a carrier pigeon in World War II, used by the RAF to send messages back home across enemy lines. On 6th June 1944, for example, he carried news back of the first D-Day landings in Normandy. He flew more than 150 miles (241km) from northern France to Portsmouth, England. His flight took just over five hours. What important D-Day message did he bring? That the allied vessels were just 20 miles off the Normandy coast, with no visible signs of German interference or counter-attack. For his work during the war he was awarded the Dickin Medal – and so takes the number of pigeons that have been awarded the medal to 32, more than any other animal, apparently.

Two great horses complete the list of animals. Warrior was a World War I horse ridden by Captain Jack Seely, serving throughout the entire war. For example, leading the Canadian Cavalry Brigade, they fought at Moreuil Wood in March 1918. Though casualties were high, Warrior escaped injury and was, too, awarded the Dickin Medal. The second great horse, Shergar, had a more unsettling story. He was a famous race horse and won many races including the Epsom Derby, Irish Derby, and Ascot races, all in 1981. To many he was a real-life equivalent to Pegasus, a winged horse from Greek mythology. With a unique white mark on his face and four white 'socks', he apparently ran "with his tongue lolling out of his mouth" (The Telegraph). But unfortunately on 8th February 1983 he was stolen from his stable by masked gunmen, never to be seen again. What actually happened to Shergar? Nobody knows for sure.

I cannot end on such a sad note, so I have added one more animal, actually a dinosaur, to the list: Dippy. He is a plaster diplodocus that for many years graced the great entrance hall, Hintze Hall, at London's Natural History Museum. He was presented to the museum by the industrialist, Andrew Carnegie, in 1905. Dippy shot to fame after he was the star of the 1975 Disney film 'One of our Dinosaurs is Missing', which followed the antics of a dinosaur who 'escaped' from the museum. Starring Peter Ustinov and Helen Hayes (amongst others), the film uses a skilful combination of suspense and humour, and is a great family movie to watch if you get the chance. Dippy will be on tour at various locations around the British Isles from 2018 to 2020 if you want to say hello.

Play: Meet the Famous Animals from Britain

Characters

Dippy, a dinosaur
Guy, a gorilla
Goldie, a golden eagle
Eros, a wild snowy owl
Belinda, a Mexican red-kneed spider
Winnie, a black bear
Brumas & Pipaluk, polar bears
Jumbo, an elephant
Unsinkable Sam, a cat
Tirpitz, a pig
Gustav, a pigeon
Warrior, a horse
Shergar, a horse
Zookeeper

Setting

A zoo with enclosures and trees.

Script

Dippy: Hello. I'm Dippy. Thank you for coming here today. I am a dinosaur. I live in the Natural History Museum. Let me introduce you to my friends...

Guy: Hello. I'm guy. I'm a gorilla. I am very big. I live in London Zoo. Everyone likes me. Would you like a banana? Ooo-ooo!

Goldie: Hello. I'm Goldie. I'm a golden eagle. I escaped from London Zoo. I live in Regent's Park. Squawk!

Eros: Hello. I'm Eros. I am a wild snowy owl. I got lost at sea, and some soldiers rescued me. Thank you! Twit-twoo!

Belinda: Hello. I'm Belinda. I am a Mexican red-kneed spider. Don't be afraid – I'm very friendly! *(no noise, but can 'spin' a web)*

Winnie: Hello. I'm Winnie. I am a black bear. Do you know Winnie the Pooh? He's my friend. Roar!

Brumas & Pipaluk: Hello. I'm Brumas. And I'm Pipaluk. We are polar bears. We are very strong. We like people – but as friends, not as dinner! Roar!

Jumbo: Hello. I'm Jumbo. I'm an elephant. I am very big. Would you like a ride on my back? Jump on! Trumpet!

Sam: Hello. I'm Unsinkable Sam. I am a cat. I live on a ship. But I float – I don't sink! Meow!

Tirpitz: Hello. I'm Tirpitz. I'm a pig. I also live on a ship. I am very heavy, but I can swim. Oink!

Gustav: Hello. I'm Gustav. I'm a pigeon. Write a letter or postcard and I will deliver it for you. Coo! Coo!

Warrior: Hello. I'm Warrior. I'm a horse. I like to fight battles, and I always win! Neigh!

Shergar: Hello, I'm Shergar. I am a race horse. I am very fast. I win races. But I disappeared. Where am I? Neigh!

Dippy: Hello again. Remember me? I'm Dippy. Thank you for coming here today.

Everyone: We love animals! We are the famous animals from Britain! Goodbye! *(everyone waves goodbye)*

(All actors take a bow)

Director's Corner

In this script, famous animals from Britain are introduced, along with appropriate animal noises. There is great scope for dressing up, and your children and teens will have great fun – it could even make a lesson in itself. The play works well with large classes, and you could have more than one of each animal, or you could add scenes such as a group of zookeepers chasing the eagle, for example. I tried to keep the sentences short and the language simple – probably more suitable for primary children than teens.

The Set
   ✓ *a sign reading 'zoo'*
   ✓ *strips of black paper to represent cages and enclosures*

Costumes and Props Box
   ✓ *various animal costumes and masks*
   ✓ *various props, eg. banana, toy ship, etc.*
   ✓ *zookeeper's costume (long coat, hat and net)*

Sound and Lighting
   ✓ *recordings of animal sounds*

Other Considerations
   ✓ *do not use real animals ;-)*
   ✓ *the theme is that all children love animals*

The Musicians of Bremen

In Brief

This is one of my favourite stories by the Brothers Grimm, and it tells the tale of four animals who, for various reasons, are discontented and decide to make their way to Bremen (in northern Germany) to become musicians.

There was once a donkey who was worked hard by his farmer, so he decided to run away to become a musician in Bremen. On the way he met a sad, sleepy dog who was also not treated well by his master. He decides to join the donkey on his was to Bremen. They meet a cat who was old and tired and could no longer chase mice. The cat was invited to join. Finally they came across a rooster crowing loudly. The donkey asked why the bird was making so much noise, to which the rooster replied that if he did not run away he would be cooked for dinner!

So, the four of them set off and after a while came across a small cottage in the middle of the forest. They looked in and saw two robbers and a table full of the most delicious food. The animals were hungry and decided to sing for their supper. However, their 'singing' was so awful that the robbers mistook it for a ghostly monster and ran away. The four animals sat down to eat.

The robbers looked at each other. Why had they run away? Were they really so foolish? They decided to go back to the house. The problem for them was that the animals saw them coming and were ready... When the robbers entered the house, the cat jumped out at them and frightened them; the dog bit them; the donkey kicked them; and the rooster flew at them. Needless to say, the robbers ran away never to return! The animals sat down and continued their meal, and lived in the little cottage forevermore.

I can see a couple of oddities with the story. The first is that the donkey is the smart one, in contrast to how the animal is usually portrayed. The second oddity is that the animals never actually make it to Bremen, and never actually become musicians! Perhaps this is to remind us that we may never reach our destination, but instead the journey is important; or that we might find something better and unexpected on the way.

Bremen is an interesting town to visit, not least because of the statue of the four animals standing on top of each other: the donkey, the dog, the cat and the rooster. Touching the front hooves of the donkey is said to make wishes come true. Bremen also has a well-preserved old town which merits at least half a day's exploration, and nearby Bremerhaven that provides a nautical flavour. Of course there is also the odor of Becks beer drifting from the brewery, but that's besides the point.

Play: The Musicians of Bremen

Characters

Donkey
Dog
Cat
Rooster
Robber 1
Robber 2

Setting

A woodland in Germany, in the middle stands a wooden house.

Script

Farmer: Work! Work! Work, donkey, work!
Donkey: Oh my goodness! This Farmer doesn't like me!
Farmer: Work, stupid donkey, work!
Donkey: Oh, no! I must run away. *(he thinks)* I know, I'll travel to Bremen to become a musician.
(he starts to walk)

***

Dog: Yawn! I'm so sleepy! I'm so old! I'm so sad!
Donkey: Why are you so sad?
Dog: My master wanted to kill me because I'm getting old. So I had to run away.
Donkey: Don't worry, dog. We can travel to Bremen together to

become musicians.
Dog: Good idea!
(they start to walk)

***

Cat: Yawn! I'm so sleepy! I'm so old! I'm so sad!
Donkey: Why are you so sad?
Cat: My master says I should chase mice, but I prefer to sit by the fire. My master was angry so I had to run away.
Donkey: Don't worry, cat. We can travel to Bremen together to become musicians.
Cat: Good idea!
(they start to walk)

***

Rooster: Cock-a-doodle-do! Cock-a-doodle-do!
Donkey: Why are you so noisy?
Rooster: Because my master wants to cook me. I don't want to be dinner! What can I do?
Donkey: Don't worry, rooster. We can travel to Bremen together to become musicians.
Rooster: Good idea!
(they start to walk)

***

Donkey: Look!
Dog: What?
Cat: What?
Rooster: What?
Donkey: A house! A robber's house!
Dog: What can you see through the window?
Donkey: I can see two robbers and I can see food, lots of food,

wonderful delicious food!
Rooster: Why don't we sing for our dinner?
Cat: Good idea!
(the four animals start to 'sing')
Animals: Ee-or, woof, meow, cock-a-doodle-do!
Robber 1: What's that?
Robber 2: A ghost!
Robber 1: Oh, no! Let's get out!
Robber 2: Run!
(they run away)
Donkey: Let's sit down and eat all this food.
Dog: Wonderful.
Cat: Delicious.
Rooster: Food!
(they eat the food)

***

Robber 1: Why did we run away?
Robber 2: We are fools.
Robber 1: Let's go back.
(they go back to the house, but...)
Cat: I will jump out at you!
Dog: I will bite your leg!
Donkey: I will kick you!
Rooster: I will fly at you!
Robbers 1 & 2: Oh, no! Run!
(they run away)
Donkey: OK, let's go back to dinner.
All animals: Cheers!!!

(All actors take a bow)

Director's Corner

Get out your animal masks or costumes again for this enjoyable play, set in the German woodlands. There are a few dramatic moments, for example the sad, tired dog explaining his story. But the highlight of drama is when the robbers return to the house only to be confronted by the animals. Try not to be too violent!

The Set
- ✓ *the German woodlands can be depicted by green leaves placed around the set*
- ✓ *a small cottage in the middle*

Costumes and Props Box
- ✓ *animal mask and / or costumes*
- ✓ *robbers' masks and / or costumes*

Sound and Lighting
- ✓ *minimal lighting is required for the set*

Other Considerations
- ✓ *don't make the fight scene too violent :-)*
- ✓ *the moral is that perhaps the journey is more important than the destination*

The Legend of the Golden Duck

In Brief

Long ago in Warsaw there was a young man, Jacob, who was known for his revelry and enjoyment of fun parties. He often told stories and jokes, and everyone liked him. However, there was no money to be made from his jokes and revelry: he was poor. One day he decided enough was enough. He decided to search for the golden duck and his fortune. He had nothing to lose.

What was the golden duck? It was a magical bird that lived in an underground pond way beneath the Ostrogoski Palace. Jacob found the palace in a valley. He soon realised it was uninhabited because in the evening there was no candlelight at the windows. So, the next day he went in to explore.

He went into the palace's dark cellar – room after room of dark, musty cellars… until he came across a cave, deep underground. What do you think he found? That's right – a golden duck! What's more, the golden duck spoke! "Hello", it said, as it glided about the water. It had fine feathers and a crest (a crown of feathers).

"Hello, golden duck" said Jacob. The golden duck replied. It explained that Jacob would be given one hundred ducats (gold coins) which he had to spend that day, and only on himself.

With his purse of one hundred ducats he started his spending spree. He bought new clothes and ate in the most expensive restaurant. The only things he had to do was keep his secret about the golden duck to himself and only spend the money on himself.

But his dreams started to get the better of him.

He looked into his purse. Only one gold coin remained. He decided to buy a cup of the finest wine, and with no money left , go back to the golden duck and claim his next one hundred ducats. However, on his way he came across a poor beggar and, as you can probably guess, gave his last gold coin to the beggar.

Suddenly, with a bang and a flash, the golden duck appeared and chanted a rhyme:

"You did not keep your word, nor our deal,
when you gave the poor beggar a meal.
And today, though you are in great need,
a poor life once again you shall lead.
Now, the goods that my gold for you bought,
In the blink of an eye will now come to nought"

Jacob could not believe his eyes. His beautiful clothes vanished, and all the fine things he had bought disappeared. Can you believe it? Jacob was left standing in his old rags once more. According to polish4kids.com, he looked at the beggar who said:

"Your good-heartedness has triumphed over greed and true treasure is not enchanted gold but a generous spirit and a pair of hands eager to work. That is the way to gain a fortune and the goodwill of others."

Jacob took this advice and worked hard to become a fine shoemaker. In fact, he made the best shoes in all of Warsaw.

To commemorate this, the people of Warsaw built a fountain in the image of the golden duck. To this day you can see this fountain (albeit a replica) in the courtyard of the palace. The enchanted golden lake is said to be way underground below it, apparently.

Play: The Legend of the Golden Duck

Characters

Jacob
Jacob's Friends
The Golden Duck
A Poor Beggar

Setting

In and around the castle and the cobbled streets of Warsaw, long ago.

Script

Scene 1: A Pub

Jacob: Let me tell you another story... Did you hear the one about the... An even funnier joke is...
Jacob's Friends: Ha ha, he he, ho ho, Jacob, you're so funny!
Jacob: Thankyou very much. But did you ever hear the funny story about the Golden Duck... Hmmm... *(he thinks to himself...) the Golden Duck...Hmmm...*

Scene 2: Ostrogoski Palace

Jacob: No-one lives in this tired old building. I will go inside. I will try to find the Golden Duck. *(he walks carefully and cautiously into the ruined building, and into the cellar)* So many rooms, so dark, so musty... will I ever find the Golden Duck?
(suddenly...)

Golden Duck: Hello! I am the Golden Duck! Quack!

Jacob: Hello, Golden Duck. My name is Jacob.

Golden Duck: Yes, I know. Quack!

Jacob: You know?

Golden Duck: I know everything. I am not stupid. I am very clever. Quack!

Jacob: Oh, OK. Can you help me make my fortune?

Golden Duck: Yes, of course. Take this purse of one hundred gold pieces. You must spend it all today, and only on yourself, Jacob. Come back tomorrow and I will give you another one hundred gold pieces. Understand?

Jacob: Understood.

Golden Duck: Be gone! Quack!

Scene 3: A Fine Restaurant, A Fine Shop

Jacob: Ha ha! Look at all this delicious food! Look at all these wonderful clothes! I will never be poor again!

Jacob's Friends: *(they look in through the window)* Ha ha, he he, ho ho, Jacob, you're so funny!

Scene 4: The Street

Jacob: Ho! I have just one gold coin left.

Poor Beggar: Hello, son. I am a poor beggar. Won't you help me? I am hungry.

Jacob: But I can't give you my last gold coin. The Golden Duck will be angry.

Poor Beggar: Golden Duck? Ha ha, he he, ho ho! Oh, son, you're so funny!

Jacob: Alright, poor beggar. Here is my last gold coin. Go and buy some food.

Poor Beggar: Thank you, son. *(he leaves)*

(suddenly – a big flash)
Golden Duck: Jacob! You betray me? Why did you give your last gold coin to that poor beggar? I told you *only* to spend it on yourself!
Jacob: Yes, but... but... but...
Golden Duck: All your fine clothes – be gone! All your delicious food – be gone! And all your money and wealth – be gone! *(suddenly all Jacob's fine things disappear in a flash, and he is left standing in his old rags)*
Jacob's Friends: Oh, Jacob, there you are! Where have you been? Another party? Come on, come with us, it's time for a drink in the pub.
Jacob: But I met a Golden Duck, and she gave me 100 gold coins, and...
Jacob's Friends: Ha ha, he he, ho ho, Jacob, you're so funny!

(All actors take a bow)

Director's Corner

The action takes place in several locations: the pub, inside the palace, a fine restaurant, and on the street. Rather than trying to build many different sets, I think it is better just to suggest some old buildings and cobbled streets and use this for all the action. Choose a confident student for the main part – Jacob – and suitably-dressed students for the other parts. There is some magic as Jacob's fine clothes disappear, which could be accompanied by a crash or flash as your actor pulls off his fine robe to reveal the original rags.

The Set
- ✓ *old buildings and cobbled streets*

Costumes and Props Box
- ✓ *Jacob's old raggy clothes*
- ✓ *Jacob's new and fine clothes*
- ✓ *a duck costume (a mask?)*

Sound and Lighting
- ✓ *maybe a flash as Jacob's clothes and wealth disappear*

Other Considerations
- ✓ *for younger actors turn the 'pub' into a 'café'*
- ✓ *the moral is to value what you have and take nothing for granted*

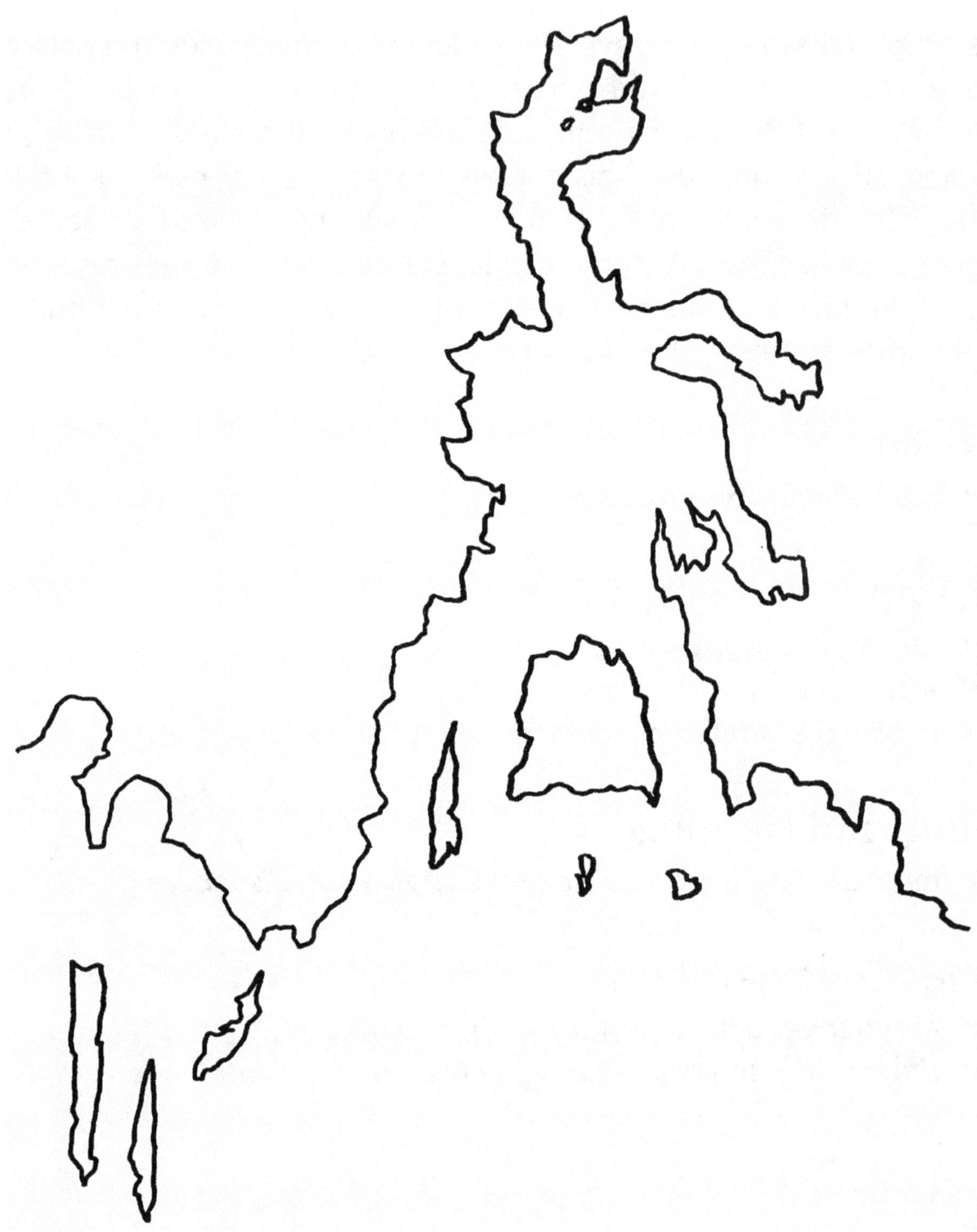

The Dragon of Krakow

In Brief

In a cave on the River Vistula lived a dragon who should never be disturbed. However some youths disturbed the dragon and it became very angry. A villager named Krakus managed to slay the dragon by baiting its food, making it drink until it exploded. Krakus was made leader of the prosperous city of Krakow.

The River Vistula has run for many centuries from the Tatra Mountains in southern Poland to the Baltic Sea at Gdansk. In its middle course is the city of Krakow and a local landmark: Wawel Hill.

There was a small village on the river near Wawel Hill. Near the village and behind an overgrown entrance lay a deep cave which many people believed to house a sleeping dragon. No-one dared go into the cave and no-one dared awaken the dragon otherwise bad things would happen to the villagers.

Youths can be short-sighted and let their curiosity get the better of them. A group of such youths went to explore the cave armed with nothing but torches. As you can probably guess, the clumsy youths awakened the sleeping dragon. They were face to face with fire, heavy breathing and anger. The dragon chased the boys out of the cave.

From that time on the dragon caused havoc in the village. It appeared from time to time and carried off sheep and young women. This became a real problem. How could the villagers be free from the dragon? What could they do?

One of the villagers, a wise shoe-maker named Krakus, had an idea. His plan was to bait the dragon's cave with sheep smeared in sulphur, a substance that would surely slay the dragon.

As luck would have it, the dragon ate the sheep and the sulphur created a terrible fire within him. To put out the fire it rushed to the river and started drinking. It drank and drank even more until finally there was a great explosion – yes, the dragon exploded!

The people of the village were happy again. Krakus was made leader of the village and soon a prosperous city grew around Wawel Hill: the city of Krakow. The 200-foot 'Dragon's Cave' ('Smocza Jama') at Wawel Hill now attracts thousands of visitors each year. Nearby runs the River Vistula that runs from the Tatra Mountains in Poland's deep south through Krakow, Warsaw and Torun, and enters the sea at Gdansk on the Baltic Sea.

What do you think? Are dragons friendly or unfriendly? What do you think a dragon looks like? Would you like to meet one?

Play: The Dragon of Krakow

Characters

Dragon
Villagers
Old folk
Youths
Krakus
Narrator
(also: cave, Wawel Hill, Vistula River, sheep...)

Setting

A small village, a long time ago, near the Vistula River and Wawel Hill.
Birds sing gently in the trees, and the river ripples quietly by the village.

Script

Villager 1: We live in a beautiful village.
Villager 2: We have our homes and our family.
Villager 3: We are happy.
Narrator: On the other side of Wawel Hill is a spooky cave.
Youth 1: Let's go into the cave.
Old Folk 1: Don't go into the cave.
Old Folk 2: A dragon lives there.
Old Folk 3: Be careful. Bad things will happen.
Youth 2: That's rubbish. Don't listen. We're not scared.
Youth 1: Come on, the cave's this way.

Narrator: A thunderstorm gathered in the background. The stupid youths went to the spooky cave with torches.
Youth 1: Here's the cave. Let's go in. *(they walk in)*
Youth 2: What's that? *(dragon snores and wakes up)*
Dragon: Roar! I am a big angry dragon. I will eat you! Roar!
All Youths: Wo-ah-ah! Run!
Narrator: The dragon chased the boys out of the cave.
Old Folk: Where have you been?
Youth 1: We went to the dragon's cave.
Old Folk: But we told you: an angry dragon lives there.
All Youths: We know!!!
Narrator: Sometimes the dragon came to the village.
Dragon: I am hungry. I will eat your sheep.
All Villagers: Oh no, it's the dragon! Run! Hide!
Krakus: Don't worry. I have an idea. The dragon likes to eat sheep. I will give him sheep with poison.
Narrator: He puts the sheep near the dragon's cave.
Dragon: Yummy! Sheep to eat!
Krakus: Look! The dragon is eating the sheep and poison.
Dragon: What? My tummy is on fire. I must drink water. Where is the river?
Narrator: The dragon drinks until it explodes. *(the dragon explodes)*
Old Folk: The dragon is gone.
Village Folk: Well done, Krakus, you saved us!
Narrator: The village grew into the city of Krakow. Everyone is happy.
Villager 1: We live in a beautiful city.
Villager 2: We have our homes and our family.
Villager 3: We are happy.
All Villagers: Hooray!

(All actors take a bow)

Director's Corner

There are a couple of very dramatic moments in the play: the first when the boys enter the cave and encounter the dragon, and the second when the dragon drinks too much and explodes. How much you make of these moments will depend on your budget and audience, but a little humour is good in any situation.

The Set
- ✓ *a village scene of cottages and trees*
- ✓ *a dark and spooky cave with a lot of rocks*

Costumes and Props Box
- ✓ *the dragon's costume can either be a simple face mask or more elaborate (and expensive) costume*
- ✓ *farmer's clothes for the villagers*
- ✓ *torches*
- ✓ *a toy sheep, or other animal, for the dragon to 'eat'*

Sound and Lighting
- ✓ *in the cave the lighting is dark and spooky, but otherwise minimal lighting*
- ✓ *an explosion sound*

Other Considerations
- ✓ *don't use a real dragon or real fire!*
- ✓ *it's interesting to study other dragons from around the world*

Greek Mythological Animals

In Brief

No country has more mythological animals than Greece – or ancient Greece to be precise. I have chosen twelve and grouped them into the good, the bad, and the ugly.

Good: *Phoenix, Pegasus, Satyr, Griffin*
Bad: *Centaur, Cerberus, Sirens, Minotaur*
Ugly: *Hydra, Chimaera, Medusa, Cyclopes*

The *Phoenix* symbolises eternal life and immortality and usually appears as a majestic eagle. It is associated with the rising of the sun and has a close relationship with the sun-god Ra. It is unusual because only one can exist at any one time. It regenerates Dr Who-style by building itself a pyre and allowing itself to be consumed by the flames. The old phoenix disappears and a new one rises from the ashes. Medieval art shows the bird as surrounded by a ring of fire.

Pegasus is a divine flying horse, usually white but sometimes gold. He is the son of Poseidon (God of the sea) and Medusa (see below). Legend has it that when Perseus beheaded Medusa, Pegasus sprang from droplets of blood from Medusa's neck. Legend also says that every time his hoof hit the earth, a spring of water emerged!

A *Satyr* was half-human, half-goat (at the rear) with animal horns. Apparently they had a flat nose and brutish expression. The Greeks often depicted them as playing flutes and drinking cups of wine – apparently the picture of a carefree life!

An interesting addition to the list is the *Griffin*, with the body and back legs of a lion, and the head, wings and front legs of an eagle. This was thought to be the powerful and majestic combination: the lion as king of beasts, and the eagle as king of birds. Depictions of griffins exist in the frescos of the Throne Room of the Palace of Knossos dating back to the fifteenth century BC. These days the griffin is used as a heraldic device, and is common in carnival processions.

Now let's turn to the bad. *Centaurs* were part-man, part-horse and so were stuck between the two worlds of human and beast. They were symbols of brute-strength. Living in mountains and forests in primal tribes, they were known for their rowdy character, accompanied by heavy drinking and other vices. This often brought them into conflict with humans. Chiron was one exception as a wise and gifted healer and respected intellectual.

Cerberus was a feared three-headed dog that guarded the entrance gates to the underworld. This 'hell-hound' was tamed by Hercules and taken into the upperworld.

The *Sirens* were beautiful but dangerous creatures, part-woman, part-fish, mermaid-like, whose beautiful and enchanting singing on cliff-tops led all passing sailors to their death.

If you came across the *Minotaur* you'd know it – with the head of a bull and the body of a man, this 'bull-man' lived at the centre of the Cretan Labyrinth. Whoever entered the labyrinth could never escape. The Minotaur was feared because it was carnivorous and man-eating. He was eventually slain by the Athenian Theseus, who entered the labyrinth but cleverly used a long yarn of string to find his way out again.

Now for the ugly. The *Hydra* was a serpent-like water beast with many heads (more heads than painters could paint), and for each head cut off it grew two more. This meant it was impossible to beat it in battle. Hercules solved this problem: after cutting off a head, he quickly burned the stump so new ones couldn't regenerate. And so the Hydra of Lerna was slain.

Chimaera was a fire-breathing monster, within the story of Homer. It had the head of a lion, the body of a goat, and the tail of a serpent.

Medusa started out as a beautiful woman with golden hair, and she vowed to give her life as a priestess of Athena. But she broke her vow when she fell in love with Poseidon, and for this Athena punished her by turning her into an ugly creature. Not only was her hair turned into poisonous snakes, but also her face turned hag-like with bloodshot eyes and green skin. What's worse, by Athena's curse anyone she looked upon turned to stone! Perseus was able to slay the beast using his highly polished shield (as a mirror, so he didn't have to look directly into Medusa's eyes) and a sword given to him by the god Hermes.

Perhaps the most feared of Greek mythological animals was the *Cyclopes*, a giant, one-eyed monster. They were a wild race of lawless creatures who possessed neither social manners nor fear of the gods. Odysseus and his men had the misfortune to come across one, who held them captive in his cave. Their fate was to be gruesomely eaten by the beast if they did nothing about it, so Odysseus hatched a plan. He got the cyclopes completely drunk, and when he was passed out Odysseus drove a burning stake into his eye making him blind. They were able to escape by strapping themselves to the underside of giant sheep and were then able to sail away to freedom.

Play: How to Kill a Mythical Beast

Characters

Narrator
Hercules
Perseus
Theseus
Hydra
Medusa
Minotaur

Setting

Ancient Greece, with the Acropolis in the background.

Script

Narrator: Beasts are big. Beasts are dangerous. Beasts are ugly. But do you know how to kill one?

Hydra: I am Hydra. I have many heads. You can't kill me – when you cut my head off, two heads grow in its place!
Hercules: Haha! I will kill you! *(he chases the monster off the set)*

Medusa: I am Medusa. I am so ugly. Look at the serpents in my hair. They will find you and eat you!
Perseus: Haha! I will kill you! *(he chases the monster off the set)*

Minotaur: I am Minotaur. I have the head of a bull and the body of a

man. Roar!
Theseus: Haha! I will kill you! *(he chases the monster off the set)*

(Hercules, Perseus and Theseus enter looking exhausted)

Hercules: Oh, I cannot kill that mythical animal, Hydra.
Perseus: I know. I can't kill that terrible Medusa.
Theseus: Me too. I can't get rid of that Minotaur!
Hercules: What shall we do?
Perseus: I know. If we all work together we can kill all three beasts.
Theseus: Great idea!
Hercules: Let's hide here behind this rock.

(they hide behind the rocks)

(Hydra, Medusa and Minotaur enter looking happy)

Hydra: Oh, those stupid humans! They will never find us!
Medusa: Yes, they will never catch us!
Minotaur: That's right, they will never kill us!

(Suddenly Hercules, Perseus and Theseus spring from behind the rock)

Hercules: Haha! You mythical beasts will die!

(The three heroes chase the three beasts around the set)

Hercules: Take that! *(he stabs a beast)*
Perseus: And that! *(he stabs a beast)*
Theseus: And that! *(he stabs a beast)*
Hydra: Oh no, I'm dead! Ahhhhh!

Medusa: Oh no, I'm dead! Ahhhhh!
Minotaur: Oh no, I'm dead! Ahhhhh!

Hercules: The mythical beasts are dead! Hooray!
(they all clap and cheer)

(All actors take a bow)

Director's Corner

There is a lot of action in this play, and it is important to have a large central area for them to take place. Your background could be as simple as cardboard hills. The final part where the heroes stab the beasts can be very dramatic – the students can over-act to their heart's content. Of course the place where you can really go to town is the costumes: Hydra has many heads, Medusa is ugly with serpents in her hair, and the Minotaur has the head of a bull!

The Set
- ✓ *a background of yellow hills with the acropolis*
- ✓ *a large central area for the fight scenes*

Costumes and Props Box
- ✓ *the beasts can have extra heads made of balloons, serpents made from stuffed socks or tights, and a bull mask*
- ✓ *plastic or foam daggers / swords*
- ✓ *a (cardboard) rock to hide behind*

Sound and Lighting
- ✓ *you could light each beast with a different colour*
- ✓ *roaring sounds for the beasts*

Other Considerations
- ✓ *make sure the students don't hurt each other*
- ✓ *the theme is that if you work together, you can achieve your goals.*

Lucky Animals of Italy

In Brief

Though there is no official national animal, the closest contender is the Italian wolf, an emblem prevalent in the capital, Rome. Ask in Florence and you'll probably get a different reply – the rooster who, in the past, saved Italy from doom. Go down to Catania in Sicily and you'll get a different answer still: the elephant! Wolf, rooster, elephant: each animal has its own tale rooted in culture and custom, providing a focus that binds together a city or community.

The *Italian wolf*, also known as the Apennine wolf, is native to the Italian peninsula. It was recognised as a sub-species of the grey wolf in 1921. Its colour is grey-brown and can weigh up to 40kg and have a body length of up to 140cm. The wolf lives mostly in the Apennine Mountains and western Alps, though they have also been found in Switzerland and southern France. In fact the wolf was widespread throughout the peninsula until the mid 1880s, and even lived as far south as Sicily. Once on the brink of extinction, the wolf population has increased from just 100 in the early 1970s to around 1,800 in 2013.

Ever since the Romans chose the wolf as their symbol, the animal has featured prominently in Italian culture and has its roots in Roman mythology: the twins Romulus and Remus were abandoned on the banks of the Tiber River when they were very young, but by some miracle a she-wolf looked after them and saved their lives. Time went by and the twins decided to found their own city. Romulus founded a walled city which he named after himself: Rome. It became very successful and its population grew; settlers from all backgrounds were welcomed and a military, judiciary and senate were established.

The image of the she-wolf who saved Romulus and Remus became the symbol of Rome, appearing on coins, public buildings and monuments, and street furniture. This is best symbolised by the she-wolf statue located in the Capitoline Museum in Rome. The bronze statue depicts the she-wolf standing, with Romulus and Remus as infants facing up to the wolf's belly. Some say the statue dates back to the fifth century BC, though it is known that the twins were a later addition. The statue and the Italian wolf it portrays have now become the symbol of Rome as 'the eternal city'.

Roosters feature prominently in Italian ceramics where they take the form of a wine pitcher. Wine is poured from the rooster's beak. How these cute and colourful jugs came about stems from 1478, the renaissance period in the Republic of Florence.

The most powerful and wealthy people were the Medici family. Their rivals, the Pazzi family, wanted to take power by an age-old method: assassination. One of the Medici family, Giuliano, had a reputation for throwing big parties and festivals for the village people, and one such festival was held in Gallina.

The Pazzi family heard of the gathering and plotted to assassinate Giuliano and his guards at the end of the party (presumably they would all be drunk and sleeping by then). But the Pazzis had not reckoned on one thing: that the fields and yards surrounding the village were filled with roosters – very noisy roosters!

At the sound of the intruders the roosters started to crow and cock-a-doodle-do like never before. Such was the din that Giuliano and his guards woke from their drunken sleep and were able to surprise the assassins and catch them. The roosters had saved them!

Giuliano was so pleased that he called for another party the next night. He ordered his artisans to make ceramic copies of the roosters in the form of wine pitchers. These were then given to all the villagers as symbols of good luck. And so the rooster brings good fortune and luck, and protects the owner from danger – especially as a house-warming or wedding gift.

One organisation that has taken the rooster as its symbol is Bari Football Club, whose proud cockerel's head looks like the one found on a well-known cereal packet.

When one thinks of Italy, the *elephant* does not immediately spring to mind. But that is exactly the symbol of the Sicilian city of Catania. The Catanian elephant is immortalised in a volcanic rock statue, "Fontana dell'Elefante", which stands in the square outside Catania's cathedral. The elephant part of the statue dates from the Roman era, while the 3.66 metre obelisk atop it is from ancient Egypt. They were joined in 1736 by architect Giovanni Battista Vaccarini who arranged them together as a fountain.

There are several stories as to how elephants became the symbol of Catania, most connected with historical links the city has with Greece and northern Africa.

At the end of the Ice Age sea levels in the Mediterranean were at an all-time low, to the extent that the islands of Sicily, Sardinia, Malta, Crete and Cyprus were (briefly) connected by land bridges. These allowed herds of animals, including elephants, to migrate to the islands. Over the centuries most of the species became extinct, though elephants developed into 'dwarf elephants'. Fossils have been found on the islands that prove this.

In Sicily at the start of the Iron Age the dwarf elephants proved very useful to the local population as they chased off wild animals and unfriendly tribes. And under Arab occupation from 831 to 1072, Catania was known as the 'City of the Elephant'.

The Catanian elephant remains the emblem of the city, and symbolises strength and long-life. Since the 1200s the local population have used elephants as a good luck charm against the fiery and unpredictable Mount Etna. You can see the elephant throughout the city — in restaurants, on palaces and public buildings, and even on the logo of the Catanian football team. Go down to the Archaeology Museum in Siracusa to see actual elephant skeletons!

So there we have it: the wolf, the rooster, and the elephant. Three unlikely friends who have each played their part in the history and traditions of Italy.

Play: The Roosters who Saved the Party

Characters

Giuliano Medici
Guards
The Pazzi Brothers
Village people
Artisans
Roosters

Setting

A small village in the Italian countryside

Script

Giuliano: Ciao. I'm Giuliano. My family is powerful. My family is wealthy. We love our village. We are kind people.
(the Pazzi brothers run in)
Pazzi Brothers: We are the Pazzi Brothers. We hate you, Giuliano! We hate the village people! We are going to kill you! Ha ha!
Villagers: Boo! Hiss! Go away!
(the Pazzi Brothers run off stage)
Giuliano: Mama mia! The Pazzi Brothers! They are not good people.
Villagers: You are a good man, Giuliano. Can we have a party?
Giuliano: Of course! Let's have one tonight in Gallina village.
Villagers: Hooray! Fantastico!

Pazzi Brothers: *(aside)* A party at Gallina village? This is our chance to kill Giuliano and his guards. Ha ha!

(later, at the party…)
Giuliano: Please eat! Please drink! Please have fun!
Villagers: This is a great party!
(they eat, drink and dance with music; finally they fall asleep; the Pazzi Brothers enter)
Rooster 1: What's that? Who's that? The Pazzi Brothers?
Rooster 2: Oh, no! We must wake Giuliano and his guards.
(they crow and cock-a-doodle-do loudly)
Giuliano: What's that? Who's that? Mama mia, the Pazzi Brothers!
Guards – kill them!
Guards: We will kill them.
(the guards and the Pazzi Brothers fight with swords)
Guards: Take that! And that!
Pazzi Brothers: Oh, no! I'm dead! *(they die)*
Giuliano: Thank you, guards.
Guards: No problem.
Giuliano: Thank you, roosters.
Roosters: Cock-a-doodle-do!
Giuliano: Thank you, village people.
Villagers: Hooray! We are safe!
Giuliano: Let's celebrate. Artisans, please make some ceramic roosters for our wine.
Artisans: Of course, Giuliano.
Giuliano: Let's have another party.
Everybody: Hooray! Fantastico!
(they eat, drink and dance with music)

(All actors take a bow)

Director's Corner

There are two big opportunities for dramatic effect in this play: the parties that Giuliano holds for the villagers, and the fight between the guards and the Pazzi Brothers. The first is fun and full of happiness and laughter, whereas the second involves fighting and death. Make the death of the Brothers as humorous or life-like as you wish!

The Set
- ✓ *an Italian village, with green hills in the background*
- ✓ *olive or lemon trees*

Costumes and Props Box
- ✓ *blue robes for Giuliano and his guards*
- ✓ *red robes for the Pazzi Brothers*
- ✓ *rooster masks*
- ✓ *toy swords and daggers*
- ✓ *wine glasses and bottles*

Sound and Lighting
- ✓ *none in particular*

Other Considerations
- ✓ *do not use real swords and daggers ;-)*
- ✓ *it is better to celebrate than to fight*

The Wooden Horse of Troy

In Brief

The story of the Wooden Horse of Troy signifies trickery in order to win a cause or battle, and echoes the saying 'beware of Greeks bearing gifts'.

But did the ancient city of Troy and the wooden horse actually exist, or is it all just a myth? Until the 1800s it was thought to be just that – a myth – until the German archaeologist Heinrich Schliemann came across what is now thought to be the remains of the ancient city of Troy. It is located near the modern-day city of Canakkale in western Turkey (Thrace).

Long ago there were a number of attempts to establish the city, but fires, invasions and earthquakes led to successive destruction. It was the seventh attempt, Troy VII, that the Greeks invaded during the Trojan War with the help of their wooden horse.

The Greeks and Trojans had fought for a long time without any success on either side. The Greek warriors had won many important battles but could not breach the sturdy walls of Troy, and neither could the Trojans drive the Greeks away. It was the Greek King Odysseus of Ithaca who had the idea to build a wooden horse. The horse was hollow and built on wheels, big enough for an army of thirty Greek soldiers to hide inside. It was built by Epeius, a master carpenter. The plan was for the Greek army to pretend to sail away in defeat, but to leave the horse (still full of soldiers) near the city of Troy.

One man, Sinon, was left behind. When the Trojans arrived to see the huge horse, Sinon pretended to be angry with the Greeks, saying that they had deserted him. He persuaded the Trojans that the horse would bring good luck, and they should offer it to the God Athena. So as to not upset the God, they dragged the horse into the city of Troy. The horse was so big that they had to tear down part of the city walls to get it in. The horse was left at the Temple of Athena as an offering to please the God. But their celebration of victory was misguided. Whilst the Trojans slept, the army of Greek soldiers rushed out from inside and killed every Trojan in sight. Their friends who had 'sailed away' in their ships came back to reinforce them and, after a big battle, the Greeks finally won.

No trace of the original horse exists, though it is possible to see reconstructions in the area today. One, at the site of Troy itself, stands around twenty metres high and is made of wooden planks. Visitors can climb a steep staircase and go inside the horse. A second reconstruction is on the seafront promenade in Canakkale. Though you can't climb up inside it, its straw-like construction is said by many to be more of a likeness to the original.

Visitors to the Thrace area of western Turkey can still see the remains of the city of Troy, though some imagination is required as the remains are incomplete and mangled. Most impressive are the remains of the walls of Troy VII; though these are only around forty metres long and five metres high, they provide a good image of the fortifications the wooden horse had to scale.

To get to Troy, the modern city of Canakkale is your starting point. You need to locate the dolmus (minibus) station below the bridge that crosses the river, then take one of the hourly minibuses to Troy (Truva). It only takes about thirty minutes. There are few facilities at the site so take a packed lunch and as the site is very exposed try not to visit if it is windy or the weather is inclement. As you enter the site a large wooden horse greets you, and after climbing up into it you can tour the city of Troy in an anti-clockwise direction. There is a small gift shop for souvenirs and guidebooks.

Play: The Trojan Horse

Characters

Greek Soldier 1
Greek Soldier 2
Trojan Soldier 1
Trojan Soldier 2
God 1
God 2
Wooden Horse
Trojan villagers

Setting

Ancient Thrace, rolling green hills and sparse trees, birds sing in the background. There is a mighty stone fortification.

Script

(Greeks stand on the left, Trojans stand on the right)

Greek Soldier 1: I hate the Trojans!
Trojan Soldier 1: I hate the Greeks!
All Greek Soldiers: We hate the Trojans!
All Trojan Soldiers: We hate the Greeks!

(the soldiers fight)

Greek Soldier 2: Let's pretend to go home in our ships.

Greek Soldier 1: Good idea.
Greek Soldier 2: We can make a wooden horse. It will confuse them.
Greek Soldier 1: We can trick them. We can win.

(the Greeks leave a wooden horse, then pretend to sail away in their ships)

Wooden Horse: Hello, I'm a wooden horse. I am not empty. I am full of Greek soldiers. We will trick the Trojans.
Trojan Soldier 1: What's this?
Trojan Soldier 2: A wooden horse.
God 1: Take the horse into your city. If you don't, we will be angry.
God 2: If you don't, we will be very angry!
Trojan Soldier 1: Let's take the horse into the city.
Trojan Soldier 2: Yes, then the Gods will not be angry.

(later, in the city...)

Wooden Horse: All the soldiers inside me are very quiet. *Suddenly...*
All Greek Soldiers: Charge! Kill the Trojans!
Greek Soldier 1: Look! Our friends from the ship are here!
All Greek Soldiers: Charge! Kill the Trojans!

(they fight and all the Trojans are killed)

All Greek Soldiers: We won! Hooray!
God 1: It was an interesting fight.
God 2: Yes, better than watching television!

(All actors take a bow)

Director's Corner

There are certainly enough characters (soldiers, Greeks, Trojans, Gods) for everyone to have a part. The only difficulty might be finding enough speaking parts: the Greeks can have lines such as "let's build a wooden horse and trick the Trojans" or the Trojans might say "what's that? A wooden horse?". Gods can be happy, authoritative or angry. There is also a lot of scope for costumes, and I suspect a lot of competition to be selected and dressed up as a God. Use old curtains or sheets as robes, and make swords and daggers from cardboard, or toy foam swords if you can afford it.

The Set
- ✓ *rolling green hills*
- ✓ *a mighty fortification (cardboard)*

Costumes and Props Box
- ✓ *Greek and Trojan costumes*
- ✓ *toy swords made from foam or card*
- ✓ *A wooden horse (cardboard)*
- ✓ *God's costume (white sheet as a robe, long beard)*
- ✓ *chairs for the Gods to sit on*

Sound and Lighting
- ✓ *a recording of battle sounds*

Other Considerations
- ✓ *be careful during the battle scene that the students don't hurt themselves*
- ✓ *be creative about how the soldiers 'appear' from the horse*

Noah's Ark

In Brief

When Noah built an ark to escape the floods, it settled on Mount Ararat in Eastern Turkey.

Mount Ararat is located in Agri Province in eastern Turkey, near the borders with Iran, Armenia and Azerbaijan. It rises to a height of 5,137 metres (16,854 feet). In fact, it is the highest mountain in Turkey, although it is only the forty-eighth highest in the world.

The story of Noah's Ark is well-known, with origins in the Bible, and I start now with a summary. God was not pleased with all the greed and crime on earth so He decided the only way to solve the problem was to destroy the earth with a severe flood. He chose Noah and his family to survive the flood, and told Noah to build a large wooden ship (an ark) that would house his family and two of every kind of animal. Of course, all the other people laughed at him, and said he was stupid to build the ark.

Noah and his family, and the animals two by two, entered the ark. Then it began to rain. It rained for forty days and forty nights, and the earth was destroyed except for those in the ark.

After one hundred and fifty days Noah sent out a dove to try to find land. When the dove came back with an olive branch Noah knew there was dry land nearby. Indeed, soon after he found dry land and Noah and his family, and all the animals two by two, left the ark to start a new life.

In the Bible, the story of Noah's Ark appears in chapters six to nine of the Book of Genesis. Apparently the ark was built from gopher wood but in reality it was probably built from cypress wood. It measured "three hundred cubits" long, "fifty cubits" wide, and was "thirty cubits" high. One cubit is forty-eight point two centimetres, so the measurement translated into metres is 144 by 24 by 14.5 metres. The ark was capable of floating with as many as 70,000 animals on board according to a study by the Department of Physics and Astronomy, Leicester University. Using the ark's dimensions, the Archimedes principal of water displacement, and approximate weights of the animals, the team were amazed to find out that the ark would have floated (reported in *The Telegraph*, 3rd April 2014).

Several researchers have claimed to have found the ark, but the Mount Ararat area is not amenable to archaeological study. Firstly, the landscape itself is rather inhospitable; secondly it is near the tense border with Armenia. From a search of the internet I was able to find two published articles with claims to have found the ark, and although they are both claims by fundamental Christians, they give us plenty of food for thought.

The first article appeared in the *Daily Mail* (28th April 2010) under the title "We've Found Noah's Ark" and features some unlikely photos of the well-preserved interior of the wooden 'ark'. The team of fifteen Hong Kong and Turkish explorers say they found seven large wooden compartments beneath snow and volcanic debris close to the summit of Mount Ararat. They claim it is built with plank-like timber, of cypress wood, each about eight inches wide, and that samples taken from the site date from 2,800 BC. Their video evidence included shots of smooth, curved walls, doors, and staircases.

Scientists remain sceptical about this "discovery", and even one of the team was quoted as saying "it's not one hundred percent that this is Noah's Ark, but we think it is 99.9 percent that this is it".

More believable is the evidence put forward in the article titled "Noah's Ark has been found. Why are they keeping us in the dark?" (sunnyskyz.com, December 13th 2013). It gives some historical background into Noah's Ark "discoveries" presented in a scientific and persuasive way.

It relates that the history of the site started in 1959 when Captain Durupinar of the Turkish army discovered an unusual shape while examining aerial photographs of the area: the shape stood out from the rocky terrain surrounding it. He sent the aerial photo to an expert at Ohio State University who concluded that the object was a ship beyond any doubt. In 1960 a group of Americans led by Captain Durupinar researched the site for two days looking for artefacts or remains. But they found nothing and concluded it was a natural formation.

Nothing more happened until 1977 when Ron Wyatt and his team started to study the site of the ark using more scientific methods (metal detectors, subsurface radar scans, and chemical analysis). They found the distance from bow to stern was 515 feet (300 cubits) and that all of the wood had been petrified. The symmetry and logical placement of the structure pointed towards a man-made object. The team discovered artefacts from within the ark such as petrified animal dung, a petrified antler, a length of cat hair, and nails and rivets far in advance of their time.

Academics are quick to pour scorn on such discoveries, saying that the expeditions are yet to produce compelling evidence and have underlying religious motivation. Is this really the site of Noah's Ark? Time will tell.

I think the academics are right to study Noah's Ark from the desk and armchair, as there is precious little for the visitor to the area to see. There are no 'ark attractions', souvenir stalls or visitor centres. The best you will find is brief mention in the region's tourist brochures. It is a shame, as so much more could be made of the location and its connection to this famous tale from Turkey.

Play: Noah's Ark

Characters

Narrator
Noah
Noah's Wife
Noah's Family (son and daughter)
God
Bad Person 1
Bad Person 2
Bad Person 3
Dove
Monkeys
Elephants
Lions
Snakes

Setting

*A bare, rocky mountain in eastern Turkey, with some small settlements.
Vegetation is mostly palm trees and scrub.*

Script

Bad Person 1: I am a bad person. I will steal your money.
Bad person 2: I am a bad person. I will fight with your friends.
Bad Person 3: I am a bad person. I will hit you and pull your hair.
God: Oh my goodness! Look at all the bad people. What shall I do?
(he thinks)

I know. I will send a great flood and kill all the bad people. But there is one good man called Noah. I will save him and his family.

Narrator: Noah and his family are working in a field.

Noah: This is hard work.
Noah's Wife: Yes, we work so hard. We are good people.
Son: Can I take a rest?
Daughter: I'm hungry!
God: Noah! Noah! Can you hear me? I am God. I will send a great flood. Build an ark. Take your family and animals two by two into the ark and you will be safe.
Noah: What? An ark? OK, let's build it.

Narrator: Noah builds an ark.

Bad Person 1: You are so stupid!
Bad Person 2: What are you doing?
Bad Person 3: I don't believe it!
Noah: I am building an ark. A big flood will come. I will save my family and animals from the flood.
Bad Person 1: Big flood? What a joke!
Bad People *(all)*: Ha Ha Ha!

Narrator: The animals board the ark two by two.

Monkeys: We are monkeys. We will be safe in the ark.
Elephants: We are elephants. We will be safe in the ark.
Lions: We are lions. We will be safe in the ark.
Snakes: We are snakes. We will be safe in the ark.
Bad Person 1: Look! It's raining!

Bad Person 2: Look! It's flooding!
Bad Person 3: Noah was right. We are drowning!
Bad People *(all)*: Ahhhhh!

Narrator: It rained for forty days and forty nights.

Noah: We are safe in the ark.
Noah's wife: Let's send out a dove to find land.
Noah: Good idea.
Dove: I will find land.
(the dove finds an olive branch)
Dove: Look! I have found an olive branch.
Noah: Yes, there must be land.

Narrator: A few days later the ark came to rest on land.

Son: We are safe!
Daughter: The water has gone!
Monkeys: We are safe!
Elephants: We are safe!
Lions: We are safe!
Snakes: We are safe!

Narrator: Noah, his family, and the animals left the ark two by two to start a new life.

Everybody: We are safe! Thank you Noah!

(All actors take a bow)

Director's Corner

The story of Noah's Ark is good to be performed as a play as it uses distinct visual imagery (ark, animals, water, mountain) and involves a lot of characters including people and animals. Preparation for your performance could involve making the stage set: different animals, rain clouds, and the ark itself. I wouldn't recommend it, but you could use real water in some form or other – for example if the play is to be performed outside.

The Set
   ✓ *a rocky mountain*
   ✓ *a large ark (either painted on paper or made of cardboard)*

Costumes and Props Box
   ✓ *a robe, stick and beard for Noah*
   ✓ *robes for Noah's wife and the bad people*
   ✓ *various animal costumes and masks*
   ✓ *an olive branch*

Sound and Lighting
   ✓ *recordings of animal sounds*
   ✓ *recording of heavy rainfall*

Other Considerations
   ✓ *do not use real animals ;-)*
   ✓ *the theme is that good will survive over bad*

Endangered! The Indian Elephant

In Brief

Elephants are adorable animals with their long trunk, tusks, and heavy ungainly body. But did you know that the Indian elephant is in great danger? Though in India they are a revered animal, there has been a steady decline in their population and increasing concerns about animal welfare.

Indian elephants are smaller than their African cousins; they also have smaller ears, a more rounded back, and a fourth toe on each back foot. Their colour is grey to brown, and they have thick, dry skin. Males (bulls) can weigh up to 11,900 pounds, while females (cows) can weigh up to 6,000 pounds. They have a lifespan of 60 to 70 years.

They have a vegetarian diet and eat grass, roots, leaves, creepers, palms, and fruit. They eat a lot: up to 330 pounds a day! They also love water and are never far away from a water source. They are fond of showering by sucking water into their trunks and spraying it on themselves. But elephants don't drink from their trunk – they just use it to pass water to their mouth.

Elephants are very sociable animals and live in a family group (a herd) of related females. This herd can vary in size from 8 to 100, and is led by the oldest and largest female. Males may live with the herd or on their own.

There is a long history of elephants in India. In the seventeenth century there were over one million elephants in the wild, and the Moghul

Emperor Jehangir had around 113,000 domesticated elephants. These days the number of domesticated elephants is down to around 3,500 and meanwhile the number in the wild is down to 30,000 – but this still ranks India as the country with the most elephants in the world. India is home to 50-60% of all Asia's wild elephants, with the largest herds in the south and north-east. One such area is the North Bank and the foothills of the Eastern Himalayas which, at 1,160 square miles, is one of the largest reserves in India.

So, what are the threats to the Indian elephant? Large areas of forest habitat are threatened in extreme by a growing human population, infrastructure projects, and clearing for cultivation. Another threat is poaching, as the elephant's precious ivory tusks fetch high prices on the black market. A final threat comes from the domestication of elephants, many of whom are used for transport, construction, logging, and ceremonies in temples. An elephant at a temple can enhance the temple's status, but these animals are often not well cared for and their work at festivals and ceremonies is hot and difficult. They are also used for begging in the city streets though conditions in the cities are unsuitable, and also put to work for tourism, in circuses and in zoos.

Though India has some of the strictest legislation in Asia, the laws are rarely adhered to or enforced.

So, what is being done to help the plight of the Indian elephant, both domestic and wild?

In 1992 the government-backed 'Project Elephant' was formed, intended to preserve habitat and establish 'biological corridors' allowing for traditional elephant migration. 25 reserves were established covering a total of 58,000km. Community-based action and building community support for conservation was seen as the key. It is also seen as important to reduce the risk and threats of poaching, such as with the project MIKE (Monitoring of Illegal Killing of Elephants). The projects have provided a valuable focus for conservation and there has been some success with the population of elephants slightly on the increase.

There is still a lot of work to do, both with wild animals and their reserves and with the welfare of domestic animals. But one thing is certain: elephants play a central role in Indian life and are closely associated with everyday religion and culture. An India without elephants is unimaginable.

Play: The Three Elephants

Characters

Indian King (narrator)
Elephant 1
Elephant 2
Elephant 3

Setting

The Indian Jungle, hot, humid and green with trees and creepers

Script

King: Hello. I'm the Indian King. I love elephants. Let's see what happened when three elephants couldn't decide where to live...

Elephant 1: Where shall we live?
Elephant 2: I'm not sure.
Elephant 3: I don't know.
Elephant 1: Let's find one place each.
Elephant 2: Then we can choose the best.
Elephant 3: Good idea.

King: So the three elephants packed their trunks and went off to find a new place...

***

Elephant 1: I am ambitious. I want to go to the city and join a temple.
Monk: Stand up! Sit down!
(the elephant stands up and sits down)
Monk: Move these boxes!

(the elephant moves the boxes)
Monk: Pull this heavy cart!
(the elephant pulls the heavy cart)
Elephant 1: I don't like this. Goodbye!
(the elephant leaves)

***

Elephant 2: I love dancing. I want to join the circus.
Leader: Dance, dance, dance!
(the elephant dances)
Leader: Jump over these boxes!
(the elephant jumps over the boxes)
Leader: Jump through this hoop of fire!
(the elephant jumps through the hoop of fire)
Elephant 2: I don't like this. Goodbye!

***

Elephant 3: I like nature. I will go to the jungle.
King: Welcome to the jungle! Please eat!
(the elephant eats)
King: Please shower yourself with water!
(the elephant showers himself with water)
King: Please take it easy!
(the elephant takes it easy)
Elephant 3: I like this! Can my friends come too?
King: Of course!
(all three elephants come to the jungle)

***

King: Who made the best choice? Do you know? Elephant 3, of course.
So let's all go and live together in the jungle nature reserve!

(All actors take a bow)

Director's Corner

You can use anything green to represent the jungle, but if time permits you could make some trees and creepers from large green paper. Other than the elephants, there are some other interesting costumes: the Indian King, monks, and a circus leader. There is a lot of action including dancing, moving heavy boxes etc, so choose lively students for these parts. The King's role is primarily as narrator, so give this part to a clear, confident speaker.

The Set
- ✓ *a hot, green jungle*

Costumes and Props Box
- ✓ *costume for the Indian King*
- ✓ *elephant costumes*
- ✓ *monk's costume (brown robe)*
- ✓ *circus leader's costume (sparkly jacket and top hat)*
- ✓ *some boxes*
- ✓ *a cart (wheelbarrow or shopping trolley)*
- ✓ *a hoop*
- ✓ *a bucket with small polystyrene pieces inside (to represent water)*

Sound and Lighting
- ✓ *recording of jungle sounds*

Other Considerations
- ✓ *the recording of jungle sounds can be played in the background throughout*
- ✓ *the moral is to find a system that works and stick with it!*

The Cat Who Came Late to the Party

In Brief

Why is there no Chinese year of the cat? Do you want the fun (mythological) answer, or the boring (factual) answer? Sometimes the myth is more interesting than the fact, so let's start with the fun answer…

Long ago lived the Jade Emperor, a divine and ancient figure who was the ruler of heaven and earth. Perhaps reasonably he found heaven the more pleasant place to live, but decided late in his reign that he really ought to visit earth. He'd heard about the strange and varied animals that lived there, and his curiosity was aroused.

So he sent a decree to the animals of the earth that a great race would be held on the following morning at daybreak. This would be through the thickest part of the forest and across the widest part of the river, to the finish line. As an incentive, the Emperor announced that he was planning to create a calendar system and would offer pride of place at the top of the calendar to whichever animal arrived first. All the animals were very excited and news of the race spread rapidly.

The cat, being the most handsome and also vainest animal (some things never change) was very interested. Its ears picked up at the thought of being at the head of the new calendar. But he also knew he was not a strong swimmer, and would need a good night's sleep before the race across the river, and an early alarm call. He turned to his friend, the rat, and asked him to wake him early the next day.

But on the day, the rat betrayed the cat and did not wake him up. Why? Some portray the rat as insecure, worried that he would seem puny compared to his feline rival. Others say the cunning, unscrupulous rat sensed an opportunity to eliminate a competitor from the race before it had even started.

You can guess what happened next, can't you? Yes, that's right – on the morning of the Imperial audience the rat arrived first and, as his reward, was given the first year in the twelve-year cycle of the new zodiac. In second place came the ox, then the tiger, rabbit, dragon, snake, horse, goat, monkey, rooster, dog, and in twelfth place the pig.

The groggy, bedraggled, and very damp cat crawled out of the river in disbelief at what his so-called 'friend' had done. There was no prize for 13th place, and there would be no year of the cat.

This tale explains why Chinese people say they were born in the year of the rat, ox, tiger, rabbit, and so on – but *not* the year of the cat. It also explains why cats chase rats: the cat was furious and swore to hate the rat forever! Millennia later our feline friends still hold a grudge about that absent wake-up call. Meow!

Oh, I'm sorry, I got carried away and forgot to tell you the boring (factual) answer. Well, cats were introduced to China from India some while after the zodiac was compiled and popularised. The original myth didn't include them at all, and the part about the rat not wanting to wake the cat was a later addition.

So, one way or another, the cat really did come late to the party!

Play: The Cat Who Came Late to the Party

Characters

The Jade Emperor (narrator)
Animals: cat, rat, ox, tiger, rabbit, dragon, snake, horse, goat,
monkey, rooster, dog, pig

Setting

The banks of a wide river in ancient China. Bamboo grows.

Script

Emperor: Hello children. I'm the Jade Emperor of Heaven and Earth. Do you want to know why there is no cat in the Chinese calendar? Let's find out…

***

Cat: Meow! I'm so clever. I'm so handsome. I am the king!
Rat: Oh, hello cat, my friend. Did you hear?
Cat: What?
Rat: There's been a message from the Jade Emperor. It says all animals are invited to a great race at daybreak. He will choose who will be in his new calendar.
Cat: New calendar? Meow!
Rat: Yes, and the first animal to cross the finish line will win, and be the

best animal.

Cat: The *best* animal? Meow! That's me, of course!

Rat: Of course, my friend.

Cat: Will you wake me up at daybreak?

Rat: Of course, my friend.

Cat: *(yawns)* I must sleep now. I will need lots of energy tomorrow.

Rat: Of course, my friend.

Emperor: I wonder who will be first. Who's this?

Rat: It is me, rat.

Emperor: Congratulations! You are the winner!

Rat: Hooray!

Emperor: Who's coming now?

Ox: It's me, ox.

Tiger: It's me, tiger.

Rabbit: It's me, rabbit.

Dragon: It's me, dragon.

Snake: It's me, snake.

Horse: It's me, horse.

Goat: It's me, goat.

Monkey: It's me, monkey.

Rooster: It's me, rooster.

Dog: It's me, dog.

Pig: It's me, pig.

Emperor: That's twelve animals. That's all. And rat, congratulations again!

Rat: Thank you.

***

Cat: *(stretches and yawns)* Meow! I'm so clever! I'm so handsome!

Rat: Hello, lazybones. Where *were* you?

Cat: What do you mean?

Rat: The Emperor came this morning. Where *were* you? Sleeping again?

Cat: What? Eh? This morning?

Rat: Didn't you hear? I'm the *best* animal!

(all other animals nod in agreement)

Cat: What? Oh no! I don't believe it! I will eat you! *(the cat chases the rat off the stage)*

***

Emperor: *(he chuckles to himself)* Hello again, children. And now you know why there's no cat on the Chinese calendar. Goodbye!

(All actors take a bow)

Director's Corner

There are a lot of animals to dress up in this play, but pride of place goes to the rat and the cat. The Chinese Emperor can stand at the side of the stage to speak, and the animals can 'race' on to stage one by one to say their lines, then form a line at the back. You might like to find some traditional Chinese music to set the scene.

The Set
- ✓ *a green background with a suggestion of grass and bamboo*

Costumes and Props Box
- ✓ *a crown, robe and moustache for the Chinese Emperor*
- ✓ *various animal costumes and masks*
- ✓ *a ribbon to denote the winning line*
- ✓ *a silver cup for the winner*

Sound and Lighting
- ✓ *some traditional Chinese instrumental music*
- ✓ *recording of clapping and cheering*

Other Considerations
- ✓ *choose the parts of the cat and rat carefully*
- ✓ *the theme is to not be too complacent about yourself*

Interesting Idioms

In Brief

Sometimes we can't quite express what we think or feel, and what's in our head or on the tip of our tongue just won't come out. This is where idioms come in: they allow us to say what we think or feel through imagery or a short and appropriate anecdote.

An idiom is something creative and poetic, used to better describe or explain an everyday situation in just a few words. Cambridge dictionary describes an idiom as "a group of words whose meaning considered as a unit is different from the meanings of each word considered separately". Similarly, Owlcation.com writes that idioms are a word or phrase in which the figurative meaning is different to the literal meaning. There are approximately 25,000 idioms in English, and many languages have equivalent or similar translations.

As native speakers we use idioms and colloquialisms without much thought, but for learners of English they can be confusing. It is figurative language that can both perplex and fascinate non-native speakers. However, knowing about their origins can help the language learner, and they are an important way to learn about local customs and culture. They are fun and appropriate to use as teaching aids, especially for students whose learning is suited to imagery and creativity.

There's a lot of idioms to do with animals, as we strive to use their innocent knowledge to explain human traits. For example 'like a fish out of water' explains the feeling that one is out of one's comfort zone, or out of one's depth. When I went to a party where I didn't know anyone, I felt like a fish out of water! Many animal idioms are to do with cats and dogs – I've included some, but in the examples below I have also made the effort to bring a larger selection of animals.

Raining cats and dogs – for when it rains especially hard – there are a couple of related explanations, probably both true, and both with their origins in medieval England. The first is that there was no refuse collection in those days and so people dumped their rubbish directly on to the street. When the streets and gutters became flooded after heavy rains these 'mini-rivers' washed away all in their path; rubbish, dead cats, dogs and all! So, heavy storms became associated with cats and dogs. The other explanation is that in medieval times thatched roofs provided the only place for animals to stay warm, but when it rained hard some of the animals would slip out of the roof space into the gutters and onto the street.

Straight from the horse's mouth – a fact, or something that can't be denied – this is funny because we all know horses can't talk! It stems from the old days when horses were the main means of transport. Dishonest tradesmen tried to sell old or low-quality horses, but canny buyers knew that you could tell a horse's age by looking at the size and shape of its teeth, ie straight from the horse's mouth.

The dog days of summer – those very hot days when it is difficult to get anything done – this idiom comes from ancient Rome. The Romans saw that the hottest days came when the dog-star, Sirius, was clearly visible. Sirius derives from the Greek *seirios* which translates to 'scorching'.

Don't count your chickens before they're hatched – don't think that something is certain until it is there in front of you and you see it with your own eyes. Similarly, *don't put all your eggs in one basket* – don't put all your hopes into one plan or project, but spread your resources and effort over a number of things.

A bird in the hand is worth two in the bush – it is usually better to stick with what you have and know rather than risk everything for something else. The idiom dates to medieval times when it was better for a hunter to have one hunting falcon in the hand rather than two similar birds out of hand in the bush. Staying with the bird theme, if you are able to solve two problems with only one action, then you have managed to *kill two birds with one stone.* And don't forget to do things in good time, because *the early bird catches the worm*!

Shed crocodile tears – to give false or fake signs of sorrow or remorse. The crocodile is often seen as an untrustworthy animal, so when it cries we put into question its true motive.

Every dog has his day – everyone will get their moment. First noted in "Erasmus' Adages" (1545) "A dogge hath a day", and later mentioned by Shakespeare in Hamlet (1603), Act 5 Scene 1 "Let Hercules himself do what he may, The cat will mew and dog will have his day". Hamlet is considered lowly by others, but he sees himself as a hero who will have his revenge – his day.

Make a mountain out of a molehill – to make a problem or situation appear bigger than it really is, and to blow events out of proportion.

Elephants never forget – If someone has done a good deed for you, you will remember and repay them in kind in the future. Similarly, if someone has done you a wrong, you will hold a grudge until you get your revenge.
However if someone has a short memory, he or she is said to have *the memory of a fish*. Apparently a fish has a memory of only seven seconds. Sorry, what did you say?

Can you think of any more animal idioms?

Play: Name That Animal Idiom

Characters

Host
Contestant 1 (George)
Contestant 2 (Mary)
Contestant 3 (John)

Setting

A TV studio decorated with lights, stars and question marks

Script

(jazzy music plays)
Host: Hello, everybody, and welcome to Name That Animal Idiom. Let's meet the contestants.
Contestant 1: Hello, I'm George and I'm from London.
Contestant 2: Hello, I'm Mary and I'm from Manchester.
Contestant 3: Hello, I'm John and I'm from Liverpool.
Host: Welcome, everybody!
(the audience cheers and claps)

Host: Let's have our first clue. If you know the answer, please press the buzzer. Are you ready?
All Contestants: We're ready!
Host: It's raining very heavily. There are lots of animals. Name that idiom!
Contestant 1: It's raining cats and dogs.

Host: That's right. Ten points.
(the audience cheers and claps)

Host: Here's the next one: you have a very short memory, about seven seconds. Name that idiom!
Contestant 2: The memory of a fish.
Host: That's right. Ten points. Here's the next one: If you start early, you get a reward. Name that idiom!
Contestant 3: The early bird catches the worm.
Host: That's right. Ten points.
(the audience cheers and claps)

Let's see the scores. Ten points each. Here's the final question. To make a problem sound bigger than it really is. Name that idiom!
Contestant 1: Count your chickens before they're hatched?
Host: No, sorry.
Contestant 2: Shed crocodile tears?
Host: No, sorry.
Contestant 3: Make a mountain out of a molehill?
Host: Yes, that's right! That makes you the winner. Well done!
(the audience cheers and claps)

Let's see what you've won... a weekend break in Liverpool, England.
Contestant 3: But I come from Liverpool, England.
Host: Oh, too bad. Join us next time on Name that Animal Idiom!

(All actors take a bow)

Director's Corner

A game show is a great opportunity to experiment with a glitzy set and jazzy music – but if resources are limited then you can do with a lot less. Similarly the host and contestants can be dressed up or just wear normal casual clothes. The host is an outgoing and enthusiastic character and many of the lines end in an exclamation mark. The idea of the play is to present animal idioms in a more light-hearted context.

The Set
- ✓ *a TV studio background decorated with lights, stars and question marks*
- ✓ *some tables or stands for the host and contestants to stand behind*

Costumes and Props Box
- ✓ *the host can be smartly dressed in suit or dress*
- ✓ *the contestants can wear a selection of different clothes*
- ✓ *a buzzer or bell for each contestant*
- ✓ *a basic scoreboard (with numbers)*

Sound and Lighting
- ✓ *a recording of jazzy music – to be played at the start and the end*
- ✓ *spotlights if they are available*

Other Considerations
- ✓ *you can change the idioms if you prefer*
- ✓ *students can write and act out their own game show*

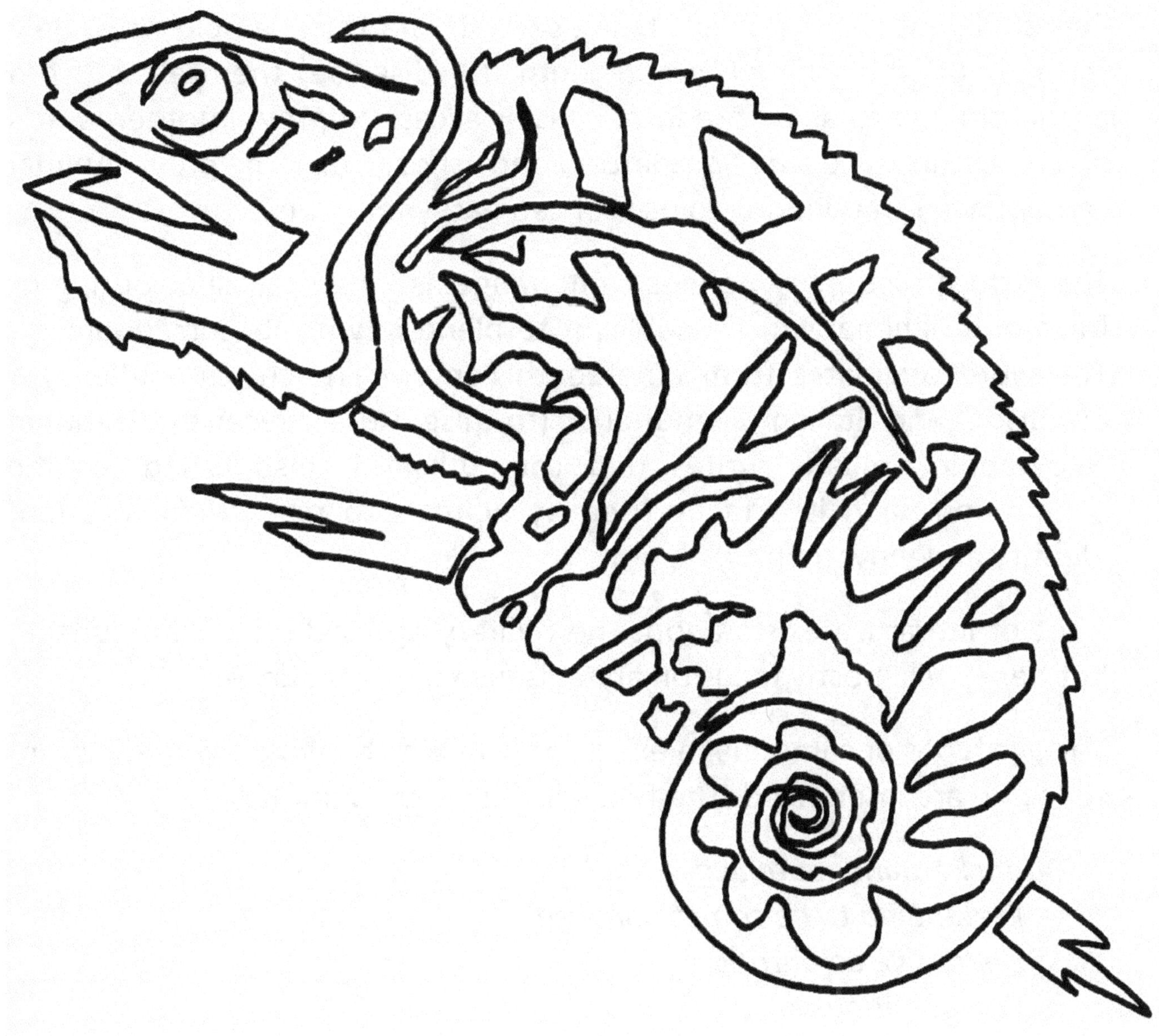

Clever Camouflage

In Brief

Camouflage is the art of not being seen. It is a tactic employed widely throughout the animal world both to disguise themselves from predators and to allow predators easier access to prey. In other words it is useful to evade predators and sneak up on prey. Animal camouflage is fascinating to us as it can easily fool human eyes.

The Oxford Dictionary defines camouflage as "the natural colouring or form of an animal which enables it to blend in with its surroundings". The word originates from nineteenth century French 'camoufler' (to disguise), and Italian 'camuffare' (to disguise / deceive). National Geographic similarly writes that camouflage is also called 'cryptic colouration', and is a tactic used by animals to mask their location, identity and movement.

A lot of literature exists about the military application of camouflage, but here I will mostly focus on animals' use of camouflage.

Various types of camouflage exist, some of which overlap venn-diagram style and are interlinked. The following list is my summary:

Background matching
Pretending to be something else
Disruptive colouration
Colour changing
Countershading
Physical features
Dazzle

Background matching is a form of mimicry when an animal resembles its surroundings in colouration, form or movement. A good example is the flounder fish which exactly matches the sand and stones of the sea floor; or the snow white coat of fur of the snow leopard; this form of disguise is very useful if the animal stays in one environment, but less so if it needs to travel through several differing habitats.

Pretending to be something else is similar to this, as animals resemble a particular part of their environment such as a twig or dead leaf. For example a dresser crab picks up pieces of coral and sponge and places them over its body so that predators can't see it. Another example is the walking leaf of south-east Asia – they even sway from side to side to mimic the swaying of a leaf in the breeze. Similarly, the leaf-tailed gecko has a tail that looks exactly like a dead leaf. My favourite is the leafy sea dragon that has flaps of skin that look like seaweed moving in the water!

Disruptive colouration is when an animal employs patterns that cause its predator to misidentify what they are looking at. Some butterflies have 'eyespots' that look like the eyes of larger animals. These eyespots misdirect and confuse. Disruptive colouration can also be used specifically for disguising an animal's shape: for example patches of light and dark colours break up the outline and shape of the peach blossom moth.

Colour changing is also used to blend into the background. Squids and cuttlefish use special muscles to control the size of the pigment cells in their skin. Chameleons are another well-known example: not only to blend in to their surroundings, but also to communicate to other chameleons that danger is nearby. The chameleon can also change the colour of its skin according to environment, mood, or state of health.

Countershading is more interesting as it really is a form of illusion. The top of an animal's body is darker in colour and the underside lighter; this shows the animal as dark where the sun would normally illuminate it, and lighter where it would normally be in shadow. This has the effect of distorting the shadow so that the animal blends seamlessly into its surroundings. Sharks, for example, when seen from above, blend into the deep water below.

Physical features of an animal can give it protection, ie their feathers, scales or fur. This 'covering' can be changed from season to season. It takes longer for some coverings to change than others: feathers and scales can be changed more often than fur. A good example of seasonal change is the arctic fox that has a brown coat in the summer and a white coat in the winter.

Dazzle is a form of illusion that uses bold, colourful geometric patterns (spots, stripes or zigzags) to obscure the target's movement – employed to great effect to paint 'dazzle ships' during the first and second world war. When an animal (or ship) employs dazzle and is in motion, it can be hard to tell what it is or how fast it is moving. Is this why zebras have vivid stripes? Zebras are social animals and live in large herds. When clustered together like this it is almost impossible to tell one from another. This makes it difficult for predators such as lions to catch they prey. Added to this is that lions are colourblind, so to them the zebra's stripes blend in to the mix of trees and scrub.

So, animals employ a variety of camouflage techniques to hide and disguise them, some quite bizarre. Animals can even fool the human eye, proving that ultimately camouflage, like beauty, may be in the eye of the beholder.

Play: The Camouflage Homework Project

Characters

Professor
Boy
Girl
Chameleon
Stick / leaf insect
Zebra
Shark

Setting

A zoo with enclosures and trees.

Script

Boy: Oh, no!
Girl: What's wrong?
Boy: We have a school project about camouflage. *(he waves his science book)* I've got no idea. What can we do?
Girl: I know. Let's go to the zoo.
Boy: Wow! Great idea!

(at the zoo...)

Professor: Hey hey! Hello children! Welcome to the zoo.
Boy & Girl: Hello. Who are you?
Professor: I'm the Professor.
Boy & Girl: We have a school project about camouflage *(he waves his science book)*. Can you help us, please?
Professor: Of course!

(they walk to the first enclosure)

Professor: Yes, yes, yes. What have we here? Oh, yes – a chameleon.
Boy: What is its camouflage?
Professor: It can change colour.
Girl: You mean, like traffic lights?
Professor: That's right.
Girl: Why does it change colour?
Professor: It changes colour to hide from other animals.
Boy & Girl: How interesting!

(they walk to the next enclosure)

Professor: Yes, yes, yes. What have we here? Oh, yes – a leafy stick insect.
Girl: What is its camouflage?
Professor: It looks exactly like a leaf.
Boy: You mean, like a tree?
Professor: That's right.
Boy: Where exactly is it?
Professor: *(looks puzzled)* I don't know. It's here somewhere!

(they walk to the next enclosure)

Professor: Yes, yes, yes. What have we here? Oh, yes – a zebra.
Boy: What is its camouflage?

Professor: It has black and white stripes.
Girl: You mean, like a crossing on the street?
Professor: That's right.
Girl: What do the stripes do?
Professor: It has stripes to dazzle the lions so they cannot see the zebras.
Boy & Girl: How interesting!

(they move to the final enclosure)

Professor: Yes, yes, yes. What have we here? Oh, yes – a shark.
Girl: What is its camouflage?
Professor: It uses light and shadow to disappear.
Boy: You mean, like a shadow puppet?
Professor: That's right.
Boy: Why does it have big teeth? Is that part of the camouflage?
Professor: No, that means it wants to eat us. Run!
(they run away)

Boy: Wow! That was great!
Girl: Yes, thanks Professor!
Professor: Hey, hey! You're welcome! Do you have enough information for your school project now?
Boy: Yes, thank you.
Professor: I have to go now. Goodbye! *(he disappears)*
Boy: Where did he go?
Girl: I don't know.
Boy & Girl: How interesting!

(All actors take a bow)

Director's Corner

It was tricky to come up with a script about camouflage, and in the end I decided the best location is the zoo. The professor and children move along the stage from one animal to the next to examine the camouflage. The boy and girl could pretend to take notes about each in their science book. Designing costumes and backgrounds for the four animals (chameleon, leafy stick insect, zebra, shark) can be a project in itself. Make sure that the costumes and backgrounds match!

The Set
- ✓ *a sign reading 'zoo'*
- ✓ *four areas of camouflage background for the four animals*

Costumes and Props Box
- ✓ *costumes for the chameleon - colourful*
- ✓ *costume for the leafy stick insect – green and brown*
- ✓ *costume for the zebra – black and white*
- ✓ *costume for the shark – blue / grey*
- ✓ *professor's robe and long beard*
- ✓ *a school science book and pencil to 'make notes'*

Sound and Lighting
- ✓ *none in particular, though you could light up each animal in a different colour*

Other Considerations
- ✓ *make sure the costumes and backgrounds match*
- ✓ *there is a lot of information about how animals use camouflage on the internet*

Herbal Remedies for Animals

In Brief

It has long been known that herbs can be an effective treatment for various human ailments and conditions, but how far can herbal remedies be used for animals? Whilst some remedies work well for both humans and animals, others can have severe negative consequences.

'Herbs' are plants that contain ingredients with active therapeutic properties, which may be present in the whole plant or just a part of it, specifically the leaf, root, stem, flower, seed, fruit, or bark. The remedy can come in many forms: teas, fresh herbs, dried herbs, oils, tinctures, flower essences, or granular extracts (as in Chinese medicine).

'Herbal therapy' is the use of herbs for medicinal or therapeutic purposes. These approaches exist as a complement for almost all conventional veterinary medicine, or simply support healing, such as the use of a tonic.

Though its use dates back centuries, it was not until the late eighteenth century that advances in science enabled chemists to isolate active ingredients in herbs. By the nineteenth century herbal therapy split from mainstream medicine, and these days the branch of medicine is called CAVM (Complementary and Alternative Veterinary Medicine) and is a fast-growing segment of the veterinary market. Herbalists argue that using their treatments produces better outcomes than conventional medicine, as well as having fewer side effects.

Shaw (1998) writes in more detail about herbal medicine, and notes it as 'complementary' to conventional medicine, noting the need for 'balance' within the body, and a 'holistic' approach: "It relies on the curative qualities of specific flowers, trees and herbs to stimulate [the] healing system and restore health... the holistic approach to maintaining good health concentrates on treating the body as an integrated system of mind, body and spirit".

Hang on a minute! This may all be very well when applied to humans, but what about animals? Can we successfully transfer some (or all) of our knowledge from humans to animals? And a lot of the literature is about dogs – how far can this be successfully applied to other animals?

Graham and Vlamis (1999) look specifically at flower essences in the treatment of animals. They argue that flowers have a "vital healing function" in animals because "they restore the balance of harmony of an animal's true nature, thereby remedying the disorders and diseases resulting from its distortion by humans...".

Petmd.com (2020) looks specifically at the use of herbal remedies for dogs. For example, they note Aloe Vera to help treat minor burns, scrapes and skin irritations due to its cooling and antibacterial properties; Calendula to treat wounds because it is anti-inflammatory and anti-fungal; Ginger to settle a dog's upset stomach; or Goldenseal, a powerful anti-biotic, used to treat eye infections. One further (and more extensive) list is provided by theherbalacademy.com (2015) who offer a chart about herbal use for animals. Below I offer a summary of the above. For those interested, Scheffer (2006) offers another list, of the 38 Bach Remedy flowers.

First and foremost in all of the literature (human or animal) is the need to consult with a professional before administering herbal medicine, and that they must be used under professional supervision (see, for example, petmd.com). Vcahospitals.com (2009) concurs that "Animal treatments are frequently inspired by human herbal medicine, but veterinary expertise is required to select the appropriate formula and to address differences in metabolism between humans and animals, and between various animal species".

So, in conclusion, what's good for humans may not be good for animals, and as vcahospitals.com puts it: "Your pets may be thought of as human, but their body systems are very different and some medicines don't cross over well".

CHART OF HERBAL REMEDIES
This is not medical advice. Always consult a professional.

Alfalfa Leaf – *arthritis, kidney tonic, nutrients*
Aloe Vera – *fleabites, minor burns and rashes, skin irritations*
Calendula Flowers – *cuts, scrapes and wounds, itch relief*
California Poppy – *relaxant, lowers blood pressure*
Catnip – *digestive aid, mild sedative*
Cayenne – *warming and circulatory stimulant, failing digestion*
Celery Seed – *antiseptic, anti-depressive, bad breath*
Chamomile – *mild sedative, stress, lowers blood pressure*
Chickweed – *cuts, eczema and itch relief*
Cinnamon – *antiseptic, promotes digestion, lifts the spirits*
Comfrey – *wounds, cuts and sprains, digestive problems*
Dandelion Root – *allergies, liver conditions, mild laxative*
Dock – *coolant, skin conditions, constipation*
Echinacea Root – *antibacterial, immune booster*
Elderflower – *cold and flu, hay fever in humans*
Eucalyptus – *respiratory problems, insect repellent*

Fennel – *tick and insect repellent*
Garlick – **not suitable for animals*
Ginger – *upset stomach, circulatory stimulant, travel sickness*
Goldenseal – *antibiotic, eye infections, stomach ailments*
Hawthorn Berry – *strengthens heart, lowers blood pressure*
Juniper – *digestive tonic, wounds, aches and pains*
Lavender – *sedative, antiseptic, flea and tick repellent*
Lemon Balm – *relaxant, insomnia, low spirits*
Mallow – *soothes and heals ulcers, digestive problems*
Milk Thistle – *protects and improves the liver*
Nettle – *allergy relief, skin disorders, cleanses blood, hair loss*
Oatstraw – *skin problems, anxiety and stress*
Oil of Wintergreen – **not suitable for animals*
Parsley Leaf – *urinary problems, fatigue, weakness, bad breath*
Peppermint – *insect repellent, motion sickness*
Sage – *antibiotic, loss of appetite, promotes long life*
Slippery Elm – *diarrhoea, vomiting, coughs*
St. John's Wort – *skin conditions, mild depression and anxiety*
Tea Tree Oil – *rids your house of fleas, mild spray for bedding*
Valerian Root – *relaxant, lowers blood pressure*
Yarrow – *skin problems, promotes healing of wounds*

Play: Good For You, Bad For You?

Characters

Host
Dog
Cat
Horse
Monkey
Fish
Human

Setting

A sparkly TV studio set with stars and lights.

Script

(jazzy music plays)
Host: Hello! Welcome to 'Good for you, bad for you'. Let's meet the contestants.
Dog: Hello, I'm Dog.
Cat: Hello, I'm Cat.
Horse: Hello, I'm Horse.
Monkey: Hello, I'm Monkey.
Fish: Hello, I'm Fish.
Human: Hello, I'm Human.

Host: OK, let's ask the first question. Are bones good or bad for dogs?
Dog: Buzz! They're good for dogs.

Host: Correct! Here's the second question. Is milk good for cats?
Cat: Buzz! It's good for cats.
Host: Correct! Here's the third question. Is straw good or bad for horses?
Horse: Buzz! It's good for horses.
Host: Correct! Here's the fourth question. Are bananas good or bad for monkeys?
Monkey: Buzz! They're good for monkeys.
Host: Correct! Here's the fifth question. Is water good or bad for fish?
Fish: Buzz! It's good for fish.
Host: Correct! Now let's ask the final question. Is alcohol good or bad for humans?
Human: Buzz! It's good for humans.
Host: Oh, no, I'm sorry! It's bad for humans.
Human: Oh, no!

Host: So, let's look at the final score. Dog has 1, Cat has 1, Horse has 1, Monkey has 1, Fish has 1, but Human has ZERO! So, the animals are the winners!
All animals: We won! Hooray! Hooray!

(All actors take a bow)

Director's Corner

This is another TV studio play, again with great scope for costumes – both the animals and the humans. Try to start and end the play with some jazzy music, like you'd hear on a cheesy TV quiz show.

The Set
- ✓ *sparkly and starry set*
- ✓ *table for the host to stand behind*
- ✓ *chairs for the contestants*

Costumes and Props Box
- ✓ *formal wear for the host*
- ✓ *a clipboard for the host*
- ✓ *animal costumes (or masks) for the animals*
- ✓ *casual wear for the human*

Sound and Lighting
- ✓ *jazzy music for the start and end*
- ✓ *spotlights and a sparkly disco ball if you can*

Other Considerations
- ✓ *don't use real animals*
- ✓ *the moral is that perhaps animals know better than humans?*

Can Birds Think?

In Brief

There's a lot of debate about whether birds can think or even show emotions. But most agree that birds do at least possess something that resembles thought or emotion.

Though birds don't communicate emotions directly, they do have a range of indirect clues that demonstrate a wide range of emotions. This is especially evident in pets, whose owners have a greater chance to bond with their birds. Owners often observe their birds' "unique moods and emotions" (thespruce.com) such as love and affection (mutual preening, sharing food, parental love), anger and rage (threatening postures, wing slaps, a chase in the air or mid-air collision), or happiness and joy (singing, sunning).

Cuteness.com similarly writes that though birds cannot communicate directly to us through speech, "their behaviours can display their emotions". They define 'emotional' as "not depending on material advantage equaling an emotional attachment", for example feeding time. They give the example of a Savannah Sparrow and a junco. The junco was recovering from a wing injury and shared a cage for some time with the sparrow. When the junco was healed and released, however, the sparrow became agitated and stopped eating. It was as if the sparrow had a broken heart!

Two academic studies are interesting in relation to birds' thought and emotion. The first is by Prof. Wasserman from the University of Iowa who studied pigeons and found that they can categorise and choose natural and man-made objects (for example 2013). In the study Prof.

Wasserman used 128 black and white photos in sixteen basic categories (baby, bottle, cake, car, and so on). The birds had to peck one of two different symbols: one a randomly-selected photo and one the correct photo. Not only did the pigeons succeed in learning the task, but they were also able to transfer their learning to new situations.

Wasserman draws a similarity between animals and humans, saying how pigeons and children learn is very similar. Pigeons were trained in all categories simultaneously, which is similar to how children learn words and categories. He concludes that the differences between animals and humans are outnumbered by similarities.

The second study, by Dr. Wilkinson at the University of Lincoln (2012), seems to concur. Apparently birds can recognise people's faces and differentiate between human voices. In the study, pigeons were shown two photos, one of a familiar person and one of an unfamiliar person. They were able to recognise and classify familiar people using only their faces as cues. Similarly the birds were able to distinguish between different human voices.

The study concluded that being able to identify a friend or foe could be the key to a bird's ability to survive: "Some humans feed pigeons, others chase them... something which could be very important for survival".

But is it 'thought' and 'emotion' or just instinct? Are the behaviours we observe emotional and heartfelt? There is a strong case for 'instinct': fear is necessary to evade predators and ensure survival; anger helps defend territory or a nesting area; and even positive emotions such as joy and love "could simply be humans viewing birds in human-like terms" (thespruce.com).

This is an interesting point which is extended on by Graham and Vlamis

(1999), who draw on the research of Prof. Coren (1994). He asks whether animals have 'personality' (which is mentalistic and implies human-like characteristics), or more simply 'temperament' (a more objective and neutral term). He notes that few people who work closely with animals doubt that they have distinctive 'personalities' and that no two animals are exactly alike, any more than two humans are.

The problem comes when we, as humans, project our own personality, characteristics, feelings and thoughts onto animals. Apparently this obscures the true nature of an animals' behaviour, and though this 'projection' can be amusing, "when we do so we no longer see them for what they are. Instead of seeing a sheep as a sheep or a horse as a horse, we see them as humans in a different form" (Graham and Vlamis, 1999).

Over time our understanding of animal and bird intelligence has improved. But are birds and animals conscious thinking beings with emotions and self awareness, or just "a bag of reflexes, automatic responses, and genetic programming, like biological machines"? (Graham and Vlamis, 1999). Can we attribute to them qualities such as love, memory, attention, curiosity, reason, shame, revenge, or even a sense of humour? Pigeons in particular appear to be smarter than your average bird; they have better eyesight than us, plus a 'homing instinct' that helps them find their way home from hundreds of miles away. A pigeon with a sense of humour is an entirely different matter.

So, can birds think? Hmmm, let me think...

I conclude that birds can think, but on a different level to humans: the eye of a pigeon could be sharper, the love of a Savannah Sparrow deeper. In the end I have to agree with thespruce.com that "the line between emotion and instinct is a thin, blurry one".

Play: Can Birds Think?

Characters

Bird, Cat, Dog, Cow, Pig, Chicken, Fox

Setting

In and around a beautiful oak tree.

Script

Cat: Hello Bird.
Bird: Hello Cat.
Cat: Can you think?
Bird: I don't know.
Dog: Hello Bird. Hello Cat.
Bird: Hello Dog.
Cat: Hello Dog.
Dog: Can you think?
Bird: I don't know.
Dog: OK, see you later!
Cat: Yes, Bird, see you later!

Cow: Hello Bird.
Bird: Hello Cat.
Cow: Can you think?
Bird: I don't know.
Pig: Hello Bird. Hello Cow.

Bird: Hello Pig.
Cow: Hello Pig
Pig: Can you think?
Bird: I don't know.
Cow: OK, see you later!
Pig: Yes, Bird, see you later!

Monkey: Hello Bird.
Bird: Hello Monkey.
Monkey: Can you think?
Bird: I don't know.
Tiger: Hello Bird. Hello Monkey.
Bird: Hello Tiger.
Monkey: Hello Tiger.
Tiger: Can you think?
Bird: I don't know.
Monkey: OK, see you later!
Tiger: Yes, Bird, see you later!

Fox: Hello Bird.
Bird: Hello Fox.
Fox: Can you think?
Bird: I don't know. What do you think?
Fox: Jump on my back and I'll tell you.
Other animals: No! No! bird! Don't jump onto the fox's back!
(but the bird flies onto the fox's back, and suddenly…)
Fox: Gulp! Yummy! Yummy!
Other animals: Oh, no! The fox ate the bird.
Fox: *(rubbing his tummy)* Can birds think? What do you think?
Growwwwl!!!

(All actors take a bow)

Director's Corner

The location of the play is in and underneath a grand old oak tree, so make some leaves and a cardboard tree trunk. Children love animals, and they can either wear a face mask, or go to town with costumes and face paint. The dramatic climax of the play is when the fox eats the bird, in the style of The Gingerbread Man.

The Set
- ✓ *leaves and a tree trunk (made of cardboard)*
- ✓ *a tank (or the whole set can be the tank?)*

Costumes and Props Box
- ✓ *face masks, or more elaborate head-to-toe costumes and face paint*
- ✓ *a bag of feathers for the 'dramatic climax'*

Sound and Lighting
- ✓ *simple lighting to light the oak tree*

Other Considerations
- ✓ *the play is very simple and can be performed without any props or costumes*
- ✓ *the play asks the children to question whether birds really can think*

References

<u>Introduction</u>
http://dictionary.cambridge.org/dictionary/english/
https://en.oxforddictionaries.com/
https://www.merrian-webster.com/
Sharman,H.E., 2004, Directing Amateur Theatre, Bloomsbury Publishing
http://www.urbandictionary.com/define.php?term=skit

<u>Paul the Psychic Octopus</u>
http://www.bbc.co.uk/news/world-europe-11626050
http://www.ibtimes.com/octopus-made-better-world-cup-predictions-goldman-sachs-photos-16113882
http://www.paulsaysyesorno.com/
http://www.thedailybeast.com/.../remembering-paul-the-psychic-octopus-germanys-world-cup-soothsayer
https://www.theparisreview.org/blog/2016/12/06/long-live-paul/
https://en.wikipedia.org/wiki/Paul_the_octopus

<u>Dick Whittington and His Cat</u>
http://www.bbc.co.uk/gloucestershire/content/articles/2005/06/16/about_dick_whittington_features_shtml
http://www.its-behind-you.com/storydickwhittington.html
http://www.purr-n-fur.org.uk/fabled/whittington.html
http://www.worldstories.org.uk/stories/story/67-dick-whittington-and-his-cat

<u>Famous Animals from Britain</u>
http://www.iwm.org.uk/history/9-famous-animals-from-the-first-and-second-world-wars
http://listverse.com/2012/08/08/top-20-world-famous-animals/
http://www.nhm.ac.uk/about-us/national-impact/diplodocus-on-tour.html
http://www.telegraph.co.uk/news/uknews/1576718/The-truth-about-Shergar-racehorse-kidnapping.html
https://en.wikipedia.org/wiki/Shergar
https://www.zsl.org/famous-animals

<u>The Musicians of Bremen</u>
https://www.bremen.de/the-tale-of-the-bremen-town-musicians-9745480
http://www.bremen-town-musicians-1
Davidson,S., 2007, The Musicians of Bremen, Usborne Publishing
Grimm,J.&W., 2018, Bremen Town Musicians, Dorlion Publishing
http://www.storynory.com/2007/08/26/the-town-musicians-of-bremen
https://en.wikipedia.org/wiki/Town_Musicians_of_Bremen

<u>The Legend of the Golden Duck</u>
https://cop19warsaw.wordpress.com
https://www.polarcenter.com/default.asp
polish4kids.com/kids-zone/legends/21-the-legend-of-the-golden-duck
https://blogs.transparent.com/polish/golden-duck-zlota-kaczka

<u>The Dragon of Krakow</u>
anglik.net/polish_legends.htm
https://discovercracow.com/wawel-dragon
https://www.myguidekrakow.com/things-to-do/krakow-dragon
https://polishtoledo.com/pagan/myths.htm

<u>Greek Mythological Animals</u>
http://www.ancient-origins.net/myths-legends/ten-mythological-creatures-ancient-folklore-001805
http://www.animalplanet.com/wild-animals/10-mythical-creatures/
Crompton, D. 2012 A Classical Primer: Ancient Knowledge for Modern Minds, Michael O'Mara Books Ltd.
Dikou-Adwera, V. (date unknown) Greek Mythology, Marmatakis Bros.
https://greekgodsandgoddesses.net/creatures/
http://list25.com/25-most-legendary-creatures-from-greek-mythology/
Mode, H. 1973 Fabulous Beasts and Demons, Phaidon Press

<u>Lucky Animals of Italy</u>
https://animalcorner.co.uk/animals/italian-wolf

http://www.bestofsicily.com/mag/art84.htm
http://brewminate.com/the-capitoline-she-wolf-romes-eternal-symbol/
http://www.historyforkids.net/romulus-and-remus.html
http://www.honestlyitaly.com/city-elephant/
https://italiannotes.com/elephants-in-catania-sicily/
https://www.italianpottery.com/2015/08/29/history-of-roosters-in-italian-ceramics/
https://www.understandingitaly.com/profile-context/italian-wolf.html
https://en.wikipedia.org/wiki/italian_wolf

The Wooden Horse of Troy
https://www.britannica.com/place/Troy-ancient-city-Turkey
https://greece.mrdon.org/trojanwar.html
https://www.historyforkids.net/greek-history.html
https://kids.kiddle.co/Trojan_War
https://en.wikipedia.org/wiki/Troy

Noah's Ark
dailymail.co.uk 28th April 2010 'We've found Noah's Ark!'
sunnyskyz.com 13th December 2013 'Noah's Ark Has Been Found'
The Telegraph 3rd April 2014 'Noah's Ark Would Have Floated'
tkcomenius.webs.com
viewzone.com/noahx.html

Endangered! The Indian Elephant
http://www.eleaid.com/country-profiles/elephants-india/
http://indiaendangered.com/interseting-facts-about-the-indian-elephant/
http://www.kaziranganationalpark.com/elephant.htm
https://www.worldwildlife.org/species/indian-elephant

The Cat Who Came Late to the Party
https://www.hutong-school.com/origin-chinese-zodiac-why-cats-and-rats-are-sworn-enemies
http://www.legendinc.com/Pages/MiscellaneousPages/Zodiak/ChineseZodiakLegend.html
http://www.topmarks.co.uk/ChineseNewYear/ZodiacStory.aspx
https://www.travelchinaguide.com/intro/social_customs/zodiac/story.htm

Interesting Idioms
http://www.bachelorsdegree.org/2011/01/30/30-common-english-idioms-and-the-history-behind-them/
https://dictionary.cambridge.org/dictionary/english/idiom
http://listosaur.com/miscellaneous/10-popular-animal-idioms-and-their-origins/
http://www.montereyherald.com/article/zz/20070806/NEWS/708069904
https://owlcation.com/humanities/Common-Idioms-and-Phrases-Meanings-and-Origins
https://www.oxford-royale.co.uk/articles/bizarre-english-idioms-meaning-origins.html

https://www.petinsuranceu.com/animal-idioms-origins/

Clever Camouflage
http://animals.howstuffworks.com/mammals/question454.htm
http://www.bbc.co.uk/nature/adaptations/Camouflage
Chatterton, M. 1998 The Utterly Nutty World of Animals Puffin Books
Hibbert, C. 2011 Really Weird Animals Tobar Ltd
http://www.nationalgeographic.com/animals/fish/I/leafy-sea-dragon/
https://nationalgeographic.org/encyclopedia/camouflage/
https://en.oxforddictionaries.com
http://www.popsci.com/what-are-the-best-disguises-in-animal-kingdom-camouflage
https://wonderopolis.org/wonder/why-do-chameleons-change-their-colors

Herbal Remedies for Animals
Graham,H. and Vlamis,G, 1999, Bach Flower Remedies for Animals, Findhorn Press
Lawless,J., 2014, The Encyclopedia of Essential Oils, Harper Thorsons
https://www.petmd.com/dog/wellness/evr_dg_herbs
Scheffer,M., 2006, Bach Flowers for Crisis Care, Healing Arts Press
Shaw,N., 1998, Herbal Medicine: A Step-by-step Guide, Element Books
https://theherbalacademy.com/basic-herbal-remedies-for-pets/
https://vcahospitals.com/know-your-pet/veterinary-herbal-therapy
https://www.vrcc.com/alternative-healing/herbal-remedies-for-animals
Westwood,C., 1991, Aromatherapy: A Guide For Home Use, Amberwood Publishing

Can Birds Think?
https://www.cuteness.com/blog/content/do-birds-become-emotioally-attached-to-people
https://www.futurity.org/pigeons-intelligence-856552
Graham,H. and Vlamis,G., 1999, Bach Flower remedies for Animals, Findhorn Press.
https://www.sciencedaily.com/releases/2012/06/120622163056.htm
https://www.thespruce.com/examining-bird-emotions-386439

Barry Nicholson is an established educator with over twenty-five years' experience teaching adults, teens and children. Born and educated in the UK, he has lived and worked in Germany, Hong Kong, South Korea, Poland, Italy and Turkey. His first book was published in summer 2015, and this book adds to his strong literary archive.

From the Same Author

Practical English Summer Camp Activities

Published June 2015   ISBN: 9780993243806

Whether you're teaching English as a foreign language or working with students who have special needs, this book provides you with over 100 enjoyable ways to engage your students in the classroom.

Famous Tales From Turkey With Activities For The Primary Classroom

Published July 2015   ISBN: 9780993243813

Twelve tales from Turkey's long and rich history, designed to enliven your class or project work, with suggested activities at the end of each section.

Famous Tales From Britain With Activities For The Primary Classroom

Published January 2016   ISBN: 9780993243820

Twelve tales from Britain's long and rich history, designed to enliven your class or project work, with suggested activities at the end of each section.

Fun Activities For Primary Children

Published February 2016   ISBN: 9780993243837

Planning a party, summer camp or extra-curricular class? Then you'll need some fun activities to liven things up and allow your children to participate and interact in a creative and informal atmosphere.

Poland In Play: Stories and Skits for ESL
Published April 2017   ISBN: 9780993243844
Poland is a fascinating and diverse country, and in this book you will find 16 stories from Poland's rich cultural history. Each story is accompanied by a play script designed for young learners.

Britain In Play: Stories and Skits for ESL
Published June 2017   ISBN: 9780993243851
Britain is a fascinating and diverse country, and in this book you will find 16 stories from Britain's rich cultural history. Each story is accompanied by a play script designed for young learners.

Children In Play
Due for publication April 2020   ISBN: 9780993243875
Who doesn't love children? Here you will find 16 stories about famous children, each accompanied by a play script that your children and teens will enjoy acting out.

www.ingramcontent.com/pod-product-compliance
Lightning Source LLC
Chambersburg PA
CBHW080516030726
47592CB00012B/3356